PRAYER:
NOT MY WILL BUT YOUR WILL

Lessons Learned When God Gave Undesirable Answers to My Prayers

Jackson Day

PRAYER: NOT MY WILL BUT YOUR WILL
Lessons Learned When God Gave Undesirable Answers to My Prayers

Jackson Day

ISBN 978-1-64370-174-5

Copyright © 2019 by Jackson Day. Permission is granted to use up to five pages of this book for non-commercial purposes provided this copyright statement is included on all pages containing material from the book: "Prayer: Not My Will but Your Will" © Jackson Day." Written permission is required for all commercial uses.

http://biblestorytelling.org

OTHER BOOKS BY JACKSON DAY

The following books by Jackson Day are available to help improve your Bible Storytelling skills:
- **Old Testament Bible Stories**   ISBN 978-0-9797324-0-9
- **New Testament Bible Stories**   ISBN 978-0-9797324-1-6
- **Bible Storytelling Tools**   ISBN 978-0-9797324-2-3
- **Key Bible Stories**   ISBN 978-0-9797324-7-8
- **Preaching With Storytelling**   ISBN 978-0-9797324-8-5

Other books by author:
- **Story Crafting**   ISBN 978-0-9797324-3-0
- **Parable Seeds: First Sowing**   ISBN 978-0-9797324-4-7
- **Parable Seeds: Second Sowing**   ISBN 978-1-64370-173-8
- **Quick Scripture Reference for Life-Issues**   ISBN 978-0-9797324-5-4
- **Outlines of Great Bible Themes**   ISBN 978-0-9797324-6-1

These books may be ordered from:
- Amazon.com
- barnes&noble.com
- Jackson Day

CONTENTS

	Page
Acknowledgments.	3
Introduction.	5
What Prayer Is.	7
What Prayer Is Not.	9
How We Should Pray.	14
God Answers Prayer.	16
Learn from the Prayers in the Bible.	27
Types of Prayer.	85
Praying the Scripture.	112
Tips to Improve Your Prayer Life.	152
Scriptural Preconditions for Believers to Receive Answers to Their Prayers.	157
Biblical Explanations of What Impedes God from Answering Prayer.	165
Reasons Not Found in the Bible Why God May Appear Not to Answer Prayers.	171
Prayer Not Answered as Requested.	177
Proper Reaction to Unanswered Prayer.	185
Prayer Activities.	195
Looking Forward.	201

ACKNOWLEDGMENTS

I understand why many authors acknowledge the help of their spouses. My wife, Doris Day, helped me tremendously with the previous books I've written. Doris was my greatest helper since we began our journey together in 1965. However, our journey together ended on December 19, 2017, when Doris experienced her birth to her heavenly life. I worked on this book during the last year of her life, but she was too sick to help me. I had the privilege of being married to the woman I loved and who showed her love to me for fifty-two years. If a good marriage is a sample of heaven, then I've been granted a foretaste of glory!

We lived in Brazil for thirty-three years. I struggled to think and write in Portuguese. As a result, my English suffered. I'm challenged when it comes to grammar and spelling, and I have writer's blindness – I see what I think I wrote instead of what I actually wrote. I'm very thankful for friends who have read the draft of this book, marked what was confusing, and gave suggestions for improving the book. They are:
- J O Terry
- Dale Weatherford
- Dr. Karen Day
- Diane Grill
- Nina Cazares
- Dr. John Ramsey
- Wade Akins
- Kristy Kennedy

I'm thankful for two university students who proofread the book to correct spelling and grammatical errors. They are:
- Whitney Jenkins
- Haley Hamer

INTRODUCTION

I'm preparing this book on prayer because I'm a student of prayer and I'm seeking to learn how to pray more effectively. I write about prayer as a fellow-struggler in the trenches. I've never found prayer to be easy. The disciples asked Jesus to teach them to pray; I'm also wanting to learn how to pray. Prayer is a difficult topic for me to write about because it is a difficult subject for me to understand and practice. I sometimes find prayer to be a time of joy and delight. I sometimes find prayer to be difficult and frustrating. I receive more negative answers to my prayers than positive ones. I find it difficult to pray for long periods of time. I run out of things to say. I don't want you to think that I write on prayer as a prayer scholar who understands prayer and is qualified to teach others about prayer. I'm struggling; I'm trying to improve my prayer life and help others to do the same.

The incident which prompted me to commence this study occurred at church. The church had been praying for a church member's son who had serious health problems. The doctors recommended a treatment, but they were not sure he would survive the treatment. However, they were certain he would die without it. Shortly thereafter, during a Sunday worship, the father informed the church that their prayers had been answered and his son was responding to treatment. Church members shouted, "Thank you Jesus," "Praise the Lord," "That is the kind of God we serve," and "Our God answers prayer." I rejoiced in hearing the father's God-story; however, I felt frustrated. I had gone to church by myself because my wife was home with complications from her illness. Also, I had a six-year-old granddaughter who had suffered from stage four cancer for five years, and her cancer has not responded to any treatment. If I had shared my God-stories of my unanswered prayers for my wife's illness and my granddaughter's cancer, there would have been no shouts of joy.

Unfortunately, I believe that the church sees winners and losers in the game of prayer. The father, whose prayers were answered, was a winner. And I, whose prayers were unanswered, was a loser. Much like a sports championship event, winners jump and shout for joy on the way back to the locker room while losers bow their heads and silently walk back to their locker room. At church, people with answered prayers joyfully share their God-stories while people with unanswered prayers suffer in silence. The church treats prayers the way doctors treat difficult surgeries. Doctors gather on the front steps of the hospital to joyfully report successful surgeries; however, they slip the corpses of failed surgeries out the back door.

I'm a student of prayer, and I'm seeking to learn how to pray more effectively. I'm a student of prayer, and I'm seeking to understand why it appears that God doesn't answer many of my prayer requests. I'm a student with a lot to learn about prayer and how to pray. I've prepared this study on prayer to improve my prayer life, and I hope it will help others improve their prayer lives as well.

WHAT PRAYER IS

The dictionary defines prayer in a general sense. Prayer is speaking to God or to an object of worship with a solemn request for help or expression of thanks. When most people think of prayer, they think of asking God for something.

People use cell phones, bluetooth devices, social media, smart phones, video chat, and talking computers to communicate with others. Prayer is the way people on earth communicate with God in heaven. Prayer is the primary way for believers in Jesus to communicate their thoughts, emotions, and desires to God, and the way to seek guidance and ask for wisdom. It is also the primary way for Christians to fellowship with God. Prayer can be audible or silent, private or public, formal or informal.

Prayer is the Christian's direct line of communication with heaven. Prayer is addressed to God the Father (Mat 6:9), done in the name of Jesus Christ (Jn 16:23), and by the enabling grace of the Holy Spirit (Rom 8:26).

The Bible describes prayer as seeking the favor of the Lord God (Ex 32:11), pouring out one's soul to the Lord (1 Sam 1:15), crying out to heaven (2 Chr 32:20), being near to God (Psa 73:28), and kneeling before the Father (Eph 3:14).

Prayer is an act, not merely an attitude. The Bible says that Jesus was praying in a certain location. After Jesus finished, one of His disciples asked Jesus to teach them to pray as John taught His disciples (Lk 11:1). Jesus began to pray, and He finished praying. Prayer involves action whereby a person begins praying and finishes it.

We should pray about everything. Paul wrote, "Do not be anxious about anything, but in every situation, by prayer and petition, with thanksgiving, present your requests to God. And the peace of God, which transcends all understanding, will guard your hearts and your minds in Christ Jesus" (Phil 4:6–7 NIV). Pray about everything; worry about nothing; yes, pray about everything.

We should pray continually. While prayer is an action that has a beginning and an ending, the Bible says to pray continually (1 Thess 5:17). We should constantly have conversations with God both day and night. The Bible does not give us a specific method of how to pray; it just tells us to pray. We should just pray under any and all circumstances.

WHAT PRAYER IS NOT

Let's take a brief look at some of the things that prayer is not, and this is not an exhaustive list.

1. **Prayer Is Not a Way to Manipulate God**

The Bible emphasizes that the primary focus of prayer is God-centered, not self-centered. True prayer does not attempt to manipulate God's power for our purpose. Such prayers are "ego-centric" prayers and are all about us. There are legitimate prayer requests that focus on individual needs or desires; but "me and mine" should not be the focus of our prayers. The person who tries to say the right words, or go through the right prayer ritual in order to get God to give him his request is not praying; he is trying to manipulate God. Those who teach that the way to get desired prayer results is to pray the "right way," are not teaching how to pray; they are falsely teaching how to attempt to manipulate God.

2. **Prayer Is Not a Format to Negotiate with God as in a Business Transaction**

The business world is immersed in the concept of Give = Get. Prayer is not telling God, "If you answer my petition, I'll do something for you in the future." For example, we don't tell God, "I'll give you my tithe money and you give me a job promotion."

I had a cousin who was an alcoholic. His daughter became seriously sick, and he tried to negotiate with God by making the promise that if God healed his daughter, he would stop drinking alcohol. Prayer is not a format to negotiate with God as in a business transaction.

3. **Prayer Is Not Putting God to the Test**

When Jesus faced His wilderness temptations, He quoted Deuteronomy 6:12 that one should not put the Lord God to the test (Mat 4:7; Lk 4:12). No one has the right to demand that God prove himself to us. The person who demands that God proves himself by providing a sign is leaving the Christian faith and entering the realm of magic. An example of putting God to the test is someone praying, "Prove to me that you are God by giving me the job I want."

4. **Prayer Is Not Some Magical Process Whereby We Call out to Some Force**

Prayer is not some kind of power with which we create things or speak them into existence, ordering God around like some servant who is in heaven. Prayer is communicating with and hearing from God. We can't summon God as though he were a genie waiting to grant our wishes. Prayer does not make demands. We can make requests of God in prayer; we dare not make demands. God is the Creator of the universe and does not take orders from us.

5. **Prayer Is Not a Wish List to the Santa Clause in the Sky**

Prayer is not a way we tell God the things we want; and therefore, we expect Him to give them to us. Jesus taught us to pray for our daily bread, so it is legitimate to pray for necessities; however, we become self-centered when we start telling God all that we desire and we demand that God give it to us. We can tell God the desires of our heart – all of them, but not for the purpose of self-gratification. We need the willingness to allow God to change and refine our desires.

6. **Prayer Is Not a Guarantee Against Suffering**

Jesus promised His disciples that, in this world, they will have trouble (Jn 16:33). Jesus prayed in the garden of Gethsemane petitioning the Father to free Him from suffering on the cross. Jesus was arrested in the garden and went to face His crucifixion. Paul prayed for God to remove the thorn from his flesh, but God gave him grace to bear it (2 Cor 12:7-10). Prayer did not prevent Jesus and the Apostle Paul from suffering, and we cannot escape suffering by praying.

7. **Prayer Is Not an Opportunity for Us to Show Off**

Jesus taught us that prayer is not an opportunity to show off in order to win praises from people (Mat 6:5). The person who prays seeking recognition from others may receive praise from people, but God isn't impressed with the prayer.

8. **Prayer Is Not a Way to Manipulate Others**

God gives people freedom of choice, which means that God does not manipulate people to force them to make the right choice.

It also means that our prayers can't force people to make the choice we desire for them to make. A young lady wanted to marry a certain young man. She got two of her friends together, and they agreed in prayer that the young man would ask the young lady to be his wife. Thus, the young lady felt that she had roped and tied him in prayer. The young wife can't use prayer to manipulate her husband to be faithful to her. Parents can't use prayer to manipulate their children to stop doing drugs. The employee can't manipulate his bosses to give him a promotion through prayer.

9. **Prayer Is Not Influencing God with the "Quantity" of Prayers**

Bombarding God with the same request several times every day does not move God to action. Prayer is not an act of collective lobbying, whereby we get a lot of people to bombard Him with our prayer request. Jesus forbade the use of constant repetition - which He called "babbling." That's what pagans do (Mat 6:7-8). The constant repetition of "spiritual-sounding" words does not make one's prayer "spiritual."

10. **Prayer Does Not Need Unnatural Language and Strange Speech Patterns**

New Testament examples of prayer involved normal talking, not a special "prayer language." When Jesus prayed, He used conversational language to talk to his Father. The name Jesus used for "Father" was the word children used to call their "Daddy." When we are praying, there is no need to use strange jargon or phrases that we would never use in normal talking to people such as, "Bless this food and the hands that prepared it," or "Traveling mercies."

11. **Prayer Is Not the Pursuit of Feelings or Experiences**

Some Christians seek to use prayer as a means to pursue intangible feelings or experiences that make them feel closer to God. In the early church, this was often the product of mixing Gnostic teachings with Scripture. More recent types tend to combine the influences of various eastern religions, such as Hinduism, and/or the occult, with the Bible.

12. **Prayer Is Not a Form of "Self Therapy" or "Spiritual Release"**

Prayer can help a sufferer feel better about his problems and himself. Comfort and encouragement often result from prayer, but that should not be the purpose of praying. Such a purpose is really no better than attempting to manipulate God for personal benefit.

13. **"Answered" Prayer Is Not a Means to Demonstrate "Spirituality"**

Many godly people did not get the answer they wanted to their prayers. The apostle Paul is such a person (2 Cor 12:7-10). And Hebrews 11:35-40 says that many people who were known for their faith did not get what they asked for. There are other issues beside answered prayer that define whether or not a person is "spiritual." The true spiritual person is the one who is willing to trust God regardless of the answer they get for their prayers.

14. **Prayer Is Not a Format for Gossip**

I've been in prayer meetings when someone used prayer as a format for gossip and to inform others about other people's problems. For example: "Lord, help Bill and Judy with their marriage problems. Lord, help deacon Joe Jones fight the tendency to have wandering eyes that lust after women."

15. **Prayer Is Not an Opportunity to Seize the Floor**

Prayer should not be seen as an opportunity to "seize the floor" and pray at great length, talking on and on and on, without fear of rebuttal or interruption. Some people get away with long boring prayers because it is considered rude to interrupt someone who is praying.

16. **Prayer Is Not a Format for Revenge**

James and John wanted to call down fire on the Samaritan village that refused to provide a place for Jesus and His disciples to spend the night. However, Jesus rebuked them (Lk 9:51-55). Revenge prayers are often heard during an election year when people pray against politicians who disagree with them. Revenge prayers are also heard during times of church conflict when church members pray against others who disagree with them. Rather than repent of personal sins, the person who prays for revenge slams or insults the person or group that he disagrees with via prayer. And he calls on God to send down a lightning bolt of judgment on them. Jesus came to save people and not to destroy them. One of the ways that we show we are children of our Father in heaven is we pray for those who persecute us (Mat 5:44-45). Jesus prayed and asked God, His Father, to forgive those who were crucifying Him (Lk 23:34). The person who prays for revenge is not inspired by the Holy Spirit; he is inspired by an evil spirit.

17. Prayer Is Not Addressed to Spirits or Demons

Prayers should be addressed to our Father in heaven, the only true Lord God, and to no one else. It is not legitimate to address prayers to unseen spirit beings and to threaten them or fight against them in order to have God gain control over a certain area or person. If you are speaking to the devil, demons, or evil spirts; you are not praying to God. On one occasion, the sound system was not working at the church and someone prayed aloud, "We command the demon who interferes with our sound system to leave this church." I've also heard prayers similar to, "We call on the demons of unbelief to flee from our presence." These were not legitimate prayers. True prayer is only addressed to God.

HOW WE SHOULD PRAY

1. **We Should Pray in Any Posture, at Any Time, in Any Place, and Under Any Circumstance**

    God does not teach us what to pray for, because we are to pray for all things and all people. "And pray in the Spirit on all occasions with all kinds of prayers and requests. With this in mind, be alert and always keep on praying for all the Lord's people" (Eph 6:18 NIV). The word "all" is repeated several times. Repetition is used in the Bible for emphasis. We are to pray on all occasions, with all kinds of prayers and requests, and for all people.

    God does not teach us the posture of prayer, because any posture will be acceptable to God. People in the Bible prayed: kneeling, lifting their eyes toward heaven, lifting their hands up, standing, sitting, lying face down, bowing, dancing, hanging on a cross, and pounding their chests.

    God does not teach us the location to pray, because any location will be acceptable to God. The Bible tells us, "... I want the men everywhere to pray..." (1 Tim 2:8 NIV). People in the Bible prayed in a closet, in a garden, while fighting, in a cave, on a cross, on a mountainside, by a river, by the sea, in a boat, in the street, in Hades, in bed, in a house, in a prison, in the wilderness, and inside a fish.

    God does not tell us when to pray, because any time will be acceptable to God. People in the Bible prayed early morning, at mid-morning, at evening, all night long, three times a day, before meals, after meals, at bedtime, at midnight, and day and night. People prayed when they were young, when they were old, and every day and always.

    How should we pray? Answer: in any posture, at any time, in any place, and under any circumstance.

2. **Prayer Is the Means by Which God Gets His Will Done on Earth, Not the Means by Which Man Gets His Will Done in Heaven**

James 5:17-18 tells us, "Elijah was a man with a nature like ours, and he prayed earnestly that it would not rain; and it did not rain on the land for three years and six months. And he prayed again, and the heaven gave rain, and the earth produced its fruit." It wasn't Elijah's asking that accomplished this but it was God answering his request because it was God's will; God had a purpose in it. God can take away things by our praying and affect people and nations, and He can add things and bless them. He can do beyond even what we ask for as we are under a covenant of grace. He can and does miracles for His namesake. We can't limit God in our prayer nor can we command Him or control Him to do what we would like by our request.

GOD ANSWERS PRAYER

God is sovereign and acts according to His will and purpose, and as it pleases Him to do so. Answered prayer is not the same as a granted request. God answers our prayers even when He denies some of our requests.

1. **God Promises to Answer People Who Pray**

God does not answer prayer; God answers people. Prayer is the means by which people make requests to God. God answers people who pray.

Psalm 91:14-16

"'Because he loves me,' says the Lord, 'I will rescue him; I will protect him, for he acknowledges my name. He will call on me, and I will answer him; I will be with him in trouble, I will deliver him and honor him. With long life I will satisfy him and show him my salvation'" (Psa 91:14-16 NIV).

Commentary:

God made promises to people who loved and acknowledged Him (Psa 91:14-16). One of the promises is, "He will call upon me, and I will answer him" (Psa 91:15). The person who loves God will pray. He has the instinct to pray, just as geese have the instinct to seek the south when the winter cold comes, or the north when the summer heat comes. God will answer the prayers of the person who loves Him. God will hear his/her petitions and grant his/her request as He considers best.

Application:

When we love God, we will pray to Him. We have the privilege of knowing that He hears us, and He will answer us according to His plans.

Isaiah 58:9

"Then you will call, and the Lord will answer; you will cry for help, and he will say: Here am I. If you do away with the yoke of oppression, with the pointing finger and malicious talk" (Is 58:9 NIV).

Commentary:
Isaiah 58 describes the way the Lord wants to be worshiped. Prophet Isaiah made a promise to the Israelites: if they combined religious observations with helping the needy and practicing social righteousness and justice (Is 58:6-7), then when they called to the Lord, he would answer (Is 58:9).

Application:
God answers us when we pray. However, one of God's preconditions to answering our prayers is that we combine religious observations with helping the needy and practicing social righteousness and justice.

Luke 11:9
Jesus promised, "So I say to you: Ask and it will be given to you; seek and you will find; knock and the door will be opened to you" (Lk 11:9).

Back-story:
Once when Jesus finished praying, one of His followers asked Jesus to teach them to pray. Jesus then taught them the model prayer, commonly called the "Lord's Prayer." Then Jesus told them the parable of a man who received a traveler into his home late at night, and he had no food for the traveler. The man went to his neighbor's house to borrow bread. The neighbor didn't want to get out of bed, but because the man kept insisting, the neighbor finally got up and gave him what he needed. The reluctant selfish neighbor in Christ's story yielded to insistent begging (Lk 11:5-8).

Commentary:
After telling the parable of the man begging his neighbor for bread at midnight, Jesus encouraged His disciples to be intense and insistent in prayer by asking, seeking, and knocking.

The words, "ask, seek, and knock," in a different context, are also found in Matthew 7:7-8, but the purpose is the same in both passages, that people should not cease to pray, and that they should pray with greater and greater urgency.

There is an ascending urgency in the successive imperatives: ask, seek, and knock. To seek is more than to ask, and to knock is more than to seek.

Jesus promised that those who ask and keep on asking, who seek and keep on seeking, and who knock and keep on knocking will experience results. This emphasized that those who are intent and insistent in prayer will be heard by God.

Application:
When it appears that God is reluctant to answer our prayer, we need to be persistent and intensify our prayer. We need to approach God with bold persistence, knowing that as a loving Father, He will provide for our needs.

Our persistence should have the purpose to search God's heart and discern what God wants for us. Persistence does not mean increasing our stubborn fixation on getting what we want or what we think is best for us.

We can be confident that God hears and answers our prayers, even when it appears that He is not listening.

John 14:13-14
Jesus promised, "And I will do whatever you ask in my name, so that the Father may be glorified in the Son. You may ask me for anything in my name, and I will do it" (Jn 14:13-14 NIV).

Commentary:
Jesus promised that those who believe in Him would do the things that Jesus was doing, and that they would do even greater things (Jn 14:12). In the context of Jesus' followers doing the things that Jesus was doing, Jesus promised to answer His followers who pray in His name. Jesus answers prayer made in His name so that the Father will be glorified. Jesus' passion was to glorify the Father; true prayer in Jesus' name has the same goal.

For one to say, "In Jesus' name", is equivalent to saying on His account, or for His sake. If a person has money and he authorizes us to draw on it, we are getting money in his name. If a son authorizes us to approach his father for help because we are his friends, we are asking for help in the son's name. The help the father gives us is because the father loves his son, and gives importance to his son's friends.

Jesus' name is not an Aladdin's lamp of prayer; it signifies both an endorsement (like a check) and a limitation (requests must agree with doing the things that Jesus did).

If believers are doing the things that Jesus did and they pray in Jesus' name, Jesus will do His part and grant what they ask. In the parallel passage (John 15:16; John 16:23), the Father is the one who answers the prayers. Both Jesus answering and the Father answering are possible because the Father and Son are one.

Application:
True prayer in Jesus' name always has the goal to honor the Father.
We pray in Jesus' name, not in our own.
If we do our part by doing the things Jesus did, then when we pray in Jesus' name, He will do His part and answer our prayer in the way it will best honor the Father.

John 15:7
Jesus promised, "If you remain in me and my words remain in you, ask whatever you wish, and it will be given you" (Jn 15:7 NIV).

Commentary:
The experience of Jesus' presence with us and His teaching influencing us (Jn 15:7), enables us to ask prayers that will give glory to the Father (Jn 15:8) and prevents us from asking selfishly for worldly things.

Jesus used a comparison from the grape vineyard to illustrate the relationship He has with His disciples. Jesus said, "I am the vine; you are the branches" (Jn 15:5). One consequence of people being connected to Jesus, in the same way as branches are connected to a vine, is they can ask for anything they want and it will be theirs (Jn 15:7). Answered prayer is a privilege of a close relationship with Jesus.

The verse has two halves: the conditions and the result. The condition: "If you remain in me and my words remain in you." The result: "ask whatever you wish, and it will be given you" (Jn 15:7). The believer who remains in Christ will have prayers that honor God rather than self. If we meet the two conditions, the result will be that we pray with power and effectiveness. Meeting the two conditions makes us into people who are devoted to bearing fruit for God's glory.

Application:
The results of living connected to Jesus and receiving His teaching make us the kind of people who are devoted to bearing fruit for God's glory, and we will pray with power and effectiveness.

Answered prayer is a privilege of our having a close relationship with Jesus and allowing His teachings to influence our lives.

1 John 3:22
"Dear friends, if our hearts do not condemn us, we have confidence before God and receive from him anything we ask, because we keep his commands and do what pleases him" (1 Jn 3:22 NIV).

Commentary:
The privilege to pray boldly to God does not give us the right to indulge in our selfish fantasies. The verse promises us that we receive whatever we ask precisely because we meet two conditions:
- We keep His commands (1 Jn 3:22). In Matthew 22:38-39, Jesus gave a summary of the commands: love God and love our neighbor. This summarizes the great commandments both of the Old and New Testaments. We believers do not earn the right to be heard by God because we obey His commandments; however, obeying God's commands gives evidence that we are His children, and God hears His children.
- We do what pleases God (1 Jn 3:22). When we consider actions that biblical commands do not deal with, we base our decisions on what will please God. Parents are disposed to give obedient and affectionate children what they desire; in the same way, God seeks to answer prayer requests of those who obey His commands and seek to please Him. We can only expect God to hear us when we live to please Him.

Application:
If we want our prayers answered, we must keep God's commandments and seek to please Him. The godly life focuses on pleasing God, even when it requires us to deny our own desires.

This verse is not a "genie in a bottle" to be rubbed and to receive whatever one desires. As we align ourselves with God's Kingdom-values, we receive what we ask for in prayer, because we desire the same things God desires.

2. **Often Believers Receive Answers Different from their Prayers**

2 Corinthians 12:7-9
"...because of these surpassingly great revelations. Therefore, in order to keep me from becoming conceited, I was given a thorn in my flesh, a messenger of Satan, to torment me. Three times I pleaded with the Lord to take it away from me. But He said to me, 'My grace is sufficient for you, for my power is made perfect in weakness.' Therefore I will boast all the more gladly about my weaknesses, so that Christ's power may rest on me" ((2 Cor 12:7-9 NIV).

Paul prayed three times asking God to remove a problem he called a thorn in his flesh. God answered, telling Paul that His grace was sufficient, and God's power is made perfect in weakness.

Commentary:
Paul doesn't say what his thorn in the flesh was, but I believe he had chronic eye problems. This is supported by a couple of things Paul wrote to the Galatians: "See what large letters I use as I write to you with my own hand!" (Gal 6:11 NIV). Paul presented big letters as his "signature style," as if to say, "you know it's me writing, because I have to write very large." Paul also wrote, "I can testify that, if you could have done so, you would have torn out your eyes and given them to me" (Gal 4:15 NIV). This probably indicates that the Galatians were sympathetic to Paul's eye problems.

These verses show us two facts concerning prayer:
- God's answer to a prayer may be different than requested. Paul had a chronic health problem that he called a thorn in the flesh. He felt that it inhibited his work and requested that God remove his affliction. However, God's response was to keep Paul humble so that his many experiences with God did not become a source of pride. God gave Paul strength to bear his affliction, thus keeping him in a

constant state of dependency on God for strength to keep going.
- God's answer to a prayer that is different than requested should be accepted. Paul accepted God's answer, even though it was not what he wanted. Paul continued his ministry despite his affliction, knowing it was fulfilling God's will.

Application:
We, like Paul, want God to remove our afflictions, especially when the afflictions are chronic and we feel that they inhibit our accomplishments.

Sometimes when we take to God a prayer request, He chooses to meet our need by giving us something different from what we asked for. And His answer may even be an undesirable one in our thinking.

I'm writing this book as my wife and I are dealing with her declining health. God has not answered our request for her to have good health or to be relieved from pain. But He is helping us deal with her declining health and frequent pain.

God often does not give us what we ask for. But, He does meet our needs.

3. **Often Believers Receive Immediate Answers to their Prayers**

Daniel 9:21-23
Prophet Daniel was praying. The Angel Gabriel appeared and told him that as soon as he began to pray, an answer was given (Dan 9:21-23).

Commentary:
An answer was immediately given to Daniel's prayer. While he was in prayer, before he had finished it, or gotten up from his knees, God's answer was sent to him.

There are other examples of immediate prayer results.
- Elisha was God's prophet in Israel. An enemy was invading Israel. The enemy king wanted to silence Prophet

Elisha, so he sent his army to where the prophet lived. Elisha's servant got up in the morning, stepped outside, and saw their town surrounded by a massive army. The servant rushed inside in a panic to tell Prophet Elisha. Elisha said, "Don't be afraid, for those who are with us outnumber those who are with them." Elisha prayed, "Lord, please open his eyes and let him see." Then the servant immediately saw that the enemy army was surrounded by an even larger army, the warriors and the chariots of heaven (2 Ki 6:8-23).
- One day, Peter and John went to the temple. A forty-year-old man, crippled from birth, was at the temple gate begging. The crippled man saw Peter and John and asked them for money. Peter said, "I have neither silver nor gold. But, I'll give you what I have. In the name of Jesus Christ from Nazareth, stand up and walk." Peter took the crippled man's right hand and helped him up. Instantly the man's legs became strong and he jumped to his feet (Ac 3:1-26).
- Saul received letters from the high priest addressed to synagogue leaders in the city of Damascus. The letters gave Saul permission to arrest any in Damascus who belonged to the Way of Christ. Saul neared Damascus and a light from heaven flashed around him. Saul fell to the ground and heard a voice saying, "Saul, Saul, why do you persecute me? I'm Jesus, the one you're persecuting. Get up! Go into the city. You'll be told what you must do." Saul was blind when he got up from the ground. God then told a disciple named Ananias to go to a certain house and ask for Saul of Tarsus. Ananias entered the house, placed his hands on Saul and said, "Brother Saul, the Lord Jesus sent me. The Lord Jesus wants you to see again and be filled with the Holy Spirit." Immediately something resembling fish scales fell from Saul's eyes, and Saul could see again (Ac 9:10-19).

Application:
    The believer who earnestly seeks God by prayer will be heard by the Lord. Sometimes, the believer receives an immediate answer to his prayer.

4. Believers May Experience Delays in Receiving Answers to their Prayers

Daniel 10:12-14

Daniel began to pray for an understanding of God's future plan for Israel. Three weeks after Daniel began his prayer, an angel told him what happened in heaven as soon as Daniel began his prayer. God's response was immediate, but the prince of the Persian kingdom prevented the actual delivery of the answer for three weeks. Then the angel explained to Daniel what would happen to the Israelites in the last days (Dan 10:12-14).

Commentary:

The delay to Daniel's prayer had to do with the prince of the kingdom of Persia. This was apparently a fallen angel assigned by Satan to the geographical area of Persia. Spiritual warfare takes place between angels who remain faithful to God and fallen angels who were cast out of heaven. And this spiritual warfare has consequences in the lives of God's people on earth.

Prayer is heard immediately in heaven, though the answer may seem to be delayed (Dan 10:13). God heard Daniel's prayer the first moment he prayed, and He immediately sent a messenger to Daniel with God's answer. However, the messenger was hindered by the fallen angel who was the angel prince of the kingdom of Persia. It was three weeks after God gave a message for Daniel that the messenger angel reached and gave Daniel God's answer (Dan 10:12-13).

Application:

Spiritual warfare impacts our lives. The conflicts between God and Satan, God's angels and fallen angels, and good and evil, impact our lives.

When we pray, God hears our prayers and determines how He will answer it; however, the answer may be delayed from causes unknown to us.

When we experience delays to our prayers, we need to keep on praying.

Luke 1:5-13
Priest Zechariah began to pray for a child when he and his bride Elizabeth were a young couple. But Elizabeth never got pregnant. Both Zechariah and Elizabeth were very old before God enabled Elizabeth to become pregnant with a son.

Commentary:
A delayed answer to prayer is not a denial. God determines the timing when a prayer is answered, and His timing is perfect.

Application:
When we pray, God hears our prayers and determines how He will answer them; however, the answers may be delayed.

Luke 18:1-8
In the Parable of the Persistent Widow, Jesus emphasized that when His followers' prayers weren't answered, they should keep on praying and not give up (Lk 18:1-8).

Commentary:
Jesus contrasted the unjust and selfish judge with the just and gracious God (Lk 18:7-8). God will respond to persistent prayer.
- Jesus also drew attention to the one area where the unjust judge and God are similar – delay. During the time when God delays, God's chosen ones cry out to him day and night (Lk 18:7).

Applications:
God may delay answering our prayers; however, our persistent continuous prayer will be answered.

5. **Believers May Have Answers to their Prayers that Go Beyond their Expectations**
"Now to him who is able to do immeasurably more than all we ask or imagine, according to his power that is at work within us" (Eph 3:20 NIV).

Commentary:
God's capacity to meet believers' needs, far exceeds anything they request in prayer or imagine by way of anticipation (Eph 3:20).

Application:
God's power is at work in us, and the manifestation of His power may exceed what we request in prayer.

I have been a long distance runner for almost 55 years. One hot summer morning I ran five miles before breakfast. I was about three miles from my home when I became thirsty. I saw a man working in his yard, and I asked him if I could drink water from his outside faucet. He answered, "I'll get you a bottle of water from the refrigerator." I had asked to drink from his faucet but he gave me a bottle of water that I could enjoy as I continued my run. He did not give me what I asked for; he gave me more.

LEARN FROM PRAYERS IN THE BIBLE

Throughout the Bible, we find records of God's people praying, and God working significantly through the prayers of His people. We can learn about prayer by studying the prayers of people who knew how to pray. When I played tennis, I always wanted to play with players who were better than me. I felt I could learn from them and improve my game. We should study the prayers of people in the Bible. This should help us learn from them and improve our prayers. Sometimes it's the structure of the prayer, sometimes it's the content, and sometimes it's the attitude of the prayer that we need to imitate.

Abraham Interceded for Sodom Genesis 18:16-33

The Lord told Abraham, "The cries of the victims in Sodom and Gomorrah are deafening; the people there are evil. I'll go down and see if they are as bad as I've heard."

The two angels who looked like men went on toward Sodom, but Abraham stood in the Lord's path, blocking his way. Abraham asked, "Will you kill the good people along with the wicked? What if there are fifty good people in the city? Won't you spare the place for the sake of the fifty good people in it? Far be it for you to kill the good with the wicked."

The Lord promised, "If I find fifty good people in the city of Sodom, I'll spare the entire city for their sake."

Abraham spoke up again, "What if the fifty fall short by five? Will you destroy the whole city because of the missing five?"

The Lord answered, "If I find forty-five there, I won't destroy it."

Abraham once again spoke, "What if only forty good people are found there?"

The Lord answered, "For the sake of forty, I won't do it."

Abraham decreased the number to thirty, then to twenty.

Then Abraham said, "May the Lord not be angry, but let me speak just once more. What if only ten good people can be found there?"

The Lord answered, "For the sake of the ten, I won't destroy it."

The Lord finished speaking with Abraham and left. Abraham returned home (Gen 18:16-33).

Back-story:
Genesis chapter 13 reports that Abraham and his nephew Lot had so many herds of animals that they could not live together (Gen 13:6), so they agreed to separate. Abraham gave Lot his choice of where he would live (Gen 13:9). Lot saw that the Jordan plain had much water (Gen 13:10), so he went there. Lot lived in the cities of the plain, and moved his tent close to Sodom (Gen 13:12). The people of Sodom were wicked (Gen 13:13).

Commentary:
Abraham started praying after he heard and understood God's words that he was going to visit Sodom (Gen 18:20).

Abraham prayed earnestly that Sodom might be spared if but a few righteous persons should be found in it.

God agreed to spare Sodom and Gomorrah if He could find ten righteous people in those cities (Gen 18:22-32). Unfortunately, ten righteous people could not be found and those cities were destroyed. However, God still answered Abraham's prayer by sending His angels to remove Abraham's nephew Lot and his two daughters before the judgment fell. So, even though the evil cities were destroyed, Abraham's prayers resulted in his family being spared (Gen 19:1-27).

Application:
We can learn from Abraham that we should feel compassion for sinners, and we should pray for them.

God responds to the prayers of His people, and our prayers can influence God's actions.

The prayer of faith acts on a knowledge of God's words and/or His will. True prayer responds to God's words and His plans. We should base our prayers on God's word, or His promises, or His warnings, or a conviction of God's will.

Abraham's Servant's Prayer Genesis 24:1-61
Abraham gave his servant Eliezer the duty of finding a wife for his son Isaac (Gen 24:1-9). He ordered Eliezer to journey to Abraham's home country, to seek a wife for Isaac among his relations. Eliezer traveled to Nahor's city (Gen 24:10). Nahor was a relative of Abraham.

Eliezer went to the town's well and prayed "O Lord, please grant me success today, and show loving-kindness to my master Abraham. The young ladies of the city are coming to draw water. When I ask a young lady for water to drink and she answers, 'Drink, and I will water your camels also'—may she be the one whom you chose for your servant Isaac."

Rebekah arrived and gave Eliezer and his camels water. Eliezer then met Rebekah's family and told them about Abraham and the duty Abraham gave Eliezer to find a wife for Isaac. Eliezer told them of his prayer and how Rebekah was the answer to his prayer. Rebekah's family agreed that she could marry Isaac, and Eliezer bowed down to the Lord (Gen 24:11-52).

Commentary:

Eliezer, Abraham's servant, asked God to give him divine guidance through providential circumstances. He prayed that when he asked a young lady for a drink of water, she would also give water to his camels. Eliezer asked for a remarkable happening that was humanly possible. A camel may drink up to 20 gallons; watering ten camels meant she would volunteer for some hard work. Culturally, providing water for thirsty travelers was an act of hospitality. But asking that a woman would also provide water for ten thirsty camels was going way beyond what would be expected. The servant's prayer "stacked the deck" against finding someone. It would take a remarkable woman to volunteer for this backbreaking task.

Before Eliezer finished praying, Rebekah came out with her pitcher on her shoulder
(Gen 24:15). God answered the servant's prayer before it was finished. The servant did not yet know the prayer was answered, but Rebekah's actions would prove it. Eliezer waited for the confirmation of his prayer, for Rebekah to give both him and his camels water (Gen 24:16-21). After Rebekah gave water to his camels, the servant ran to meet Rebekah and then he spoke to her family.

This Bible story records no word from God, no miracle, no prophetic oracle. But it gives evidence of God sovereignly working through the circumstances of those who are acting in faith. The servant looked at ordinary events with eyes of faith and professed that God led him by the right way to accomplish his employer's charge to him (Gen 24:48).

Application:
We need to act similarly to Abraham and his servant. We need to both, claim God's promises and act to ensure that His kingdom's program continues in our lives.

God sometimes demonstrates His power by answering prayer before or as we're praying.

Prayer is no substitute for action. The servant prayed. Then he observed Rebekah's actions, and then he ran to meet her and spoke to her family.

God is a personal God who is committed to and involved in the lives of His servants. He is involved in our life events, such as the challenge of finding a suitable life-partner.

Jacob's Prayer Genesis 32:9-12

Jacob was afraid. Jacob was returning to the land of his brother Esau. Jacob had deceived their father Isaac into giving him his brother Esau's blessing. Jacob was obeying God in returning to Canaan, but he was terrified.

On the way back home, Jacob prayed, "O God of my father Abraham, God of my father Isaac, Lord, you who said to me, 'Go back to your country and your relatives, and I will make you prosper,' I am unworthy of all the kindness and faithfulness you have shown your servant. I had only my staff when I crossed this Jordan, but now I have become two camps. Save me, I pray, from the hand of my brother Esau, for I am afraid he will come and attack me, and also the mothers of my children and my children. But you have said, 'I will surely make you prosper and will make your descendants like the sand of the sea which cannot be counted'" (Gen 32:9-12 NIV).

Commentary:
Notice how Jacob repeated himself and twice reminded God about this promise to prosper him. He also reminded God to consider his wives and children. He humbled himself. He acknowledged how God had blessed him abundantly and how unworthy he was of God's great faithfulness to him. He addressed God as the God of Abraham and Isaac.

Jacob took action to do what he could do. He divided his camp into two groups. In the event one group was attacked, hopefully the other would survive. That shows the distress Jacob felt at the prospect of meeting his brother after so many years. Finally, he sends his wives, maids, children and possessions across the river until he is by himself. Jacob was by himself, and a man wrestled with him until daybreak (Gen 32:24).

Then Jacob prayed, affirmed God's promises, confessed he was unworthy of God's blessings, and requested for God to do what only He could do – save him from his brother.

Application:
A crisis can often strip away our pretenses and self-confidence. A crisis can bring us to face our wrongdoing that we would rather not confront, and turn to God in desperation.

In times of crisis, we need to take action to do what we can do, and we also need to pray for God to do what only He can do.

Job's Prayer Job 42:2-6

Job spoke to God, "I know that you can do all things; no purpose of yours can be thwarted. You asked, 'Who is this that obscures my plans without knowledge?' Surely I spoke of things I did not understand, things too wonderful for me to know. You said, 'Listen now, and I will speak; I will question you, and you shall answer me.' My ears had heard of you but now my eyes have seen you. Therefore I despise myself and repent in dust and ashes" (Job 42:2-6 NIV).

Commentary:
Job did not ask God for anything in his prayer. Job's prayer ends with his confession, "Therefore I despise myself and repent in dust and ashes" (Job 42:6 NIV).

At the beginning of Job's story, Job was greatly blessed and extravagantly wealthy. Job served God unreservedly. Satan accused Job of only serving God because of the way God blessed him. Satan told God, "Job doesn't fear God for anything. You have put a hedge around him and his household and everything he has. You have blessed everything he does. His flocks and herds are spread throughout the land" (Job 1:9-10).

God allowed a severe testing of Job in which blessing by blessing was stripped away from his life. When the worst calamity hit Job, his wife urged him to, "Curse God and die!" (Job 2:9).

Job did not listen to his wife. Neither did he agree with his friends who came, first to comfort him and then to blame Job with accusations that Job's problems were the consequences of his own wrongdoings. Job insisted upon his own innocence. Job didn't understand why he experienced calamities, but Job still clung to God. Job told his friends, "Though God kills me, yet will I hope in him; however, I will defend my behavior to his face" (Job 13:15).

Job's friends argued with Job to admit that he must have sinned in some way to bring these consequences. Job argued with them to trust in his innocence and his right standing before God.

In the end, God asked Job "I will ask you, and you teach me. Will you condemn me so that you may be justified?" (Job 40:8).

Job reached the point to where he discontinued justifying himself; instead, he acknowledged the superior greatness of God.

Application:
Most of us will not face crisis and testing trials like Job. We will face unexpected downturns in our lives when we do not understand why bad things are happening to us. When we don't understand, we need to get to the place where Job arrived. We may question why God does not appear to be faithful to us, or why He appears to be silent as we suffer. We may argue our case and try to understand. But we also need to pray Job's prayer. When prayer is unanswered, we must not demean ourselves, doubt our faith, or deny God's goodness. Rather, we should model ourselves after Job, who experienced heart-wrenching unanswered prayers. In spite of that, he declared that even if God killed him, he would still hope in God (Job 13:15). That's faith!

Moses' Prayer Exodus 32:7-14
God miraculously answered many of Moses' prayers. Moses prayed, and God parted the Red Sea (Exodus 14:13-22). Moses prayed, and God gave the Israelites good water in the wilderness (Exodus 15:25). The most miraculous answer that God gave to Moses was when Moses prayed that God would spare Israel after the incident with the golden calf (Exodus 32:7-14).

After giving the Ten Commandments to the Israelites, Moses returned to the mountain top and stayed there for forty days (Ex 24:12-18).

The Israelites saw that Moses stayed on the mountain top for a long time. They confronted Aaron, "Make us gods who will go before us. We don't know what happened to Moses, the one who led us out of Egypt."

The people took off their earrings. Aaron took the gold, melted it, and used an engraving tool to make an idol in the shape of a calf.

The people shouted, "Oh Israel! These are your gods who brought you out of Egypt."

Aaron built an altar in front of the idol and said, "Tomorrow, we'll have a festival in the Lord's honor."

The next day the people offered animals as burnt offerings. They sat down to eat and drink, and got up to dance and engage in sexual activity (Ex 32:1-6 NIV).

The Lord told Moses, "Get down there! Your people, whom you brought up out of Egypt, have become corrupt. They've turned away from what I commanded them. They made an idol cast in the shape of a calf. They bowed down to it, sacrificed to it and said, `These are your gods, oh Israel, who brought you up out of the land of Egypt.' These people are a stubborn, hard-headed people! Now give my anger free reign to burst into flames and destroy them. Then I'll make you into a great nation."

Moses begged, "Oh Lord, don't let your anger destroy your people. You brought them out of Egypt with your great power and strength. Why let the Egyptians say, 'He brought them out, only to kill them in the mountains?' Don't bring disaster on your people! Remember your servants Abraham, Isaac, and Israel, who was also called Jacob. You gave them your word, telling them, `I'll make your descendants as numerous as the stars in the sky. I'll give your descendants all this land that I promised them, and it will be theirs forever.'"

The Lord reconsidered and decided not to destroy the people (Ex 32:7-14 NIV).

Commentary:

God told Moses that he was going to destroy the nation of Israel, and reconstruct the nation from Moses' own offspring. Moses himself was a descendant of Abraham, Isaac, and Jacob; therefore, God's promises to the patriarchs would have been fulfilled.

Moses, in his prayer, took God's interests into his heart as his own. Moses appealed to God, boldly interceding for the people of Israel, pleading for mercy rather than destruction for them. And God relented and responded positively to Moses' prayer.

The basis of Moses' prayer appeals were:
- Because the people of Israel were God's own people: "Why should your anger burn against your people, whom you brought out of Egypt... ?" (Ex 32:11).
- Because of God's name and reputation: "Why should the Egyptians say, 'It was with evil intent that he brought them out, to kill them in the mountains and to wipe them off the face of the earth'"? (Ex 32:12).
- Because of God's reputation: "If you put these people to death all at one time, the nations...will say, 'The Lord was not able to bring these people into the land he promised them on oath; so he slaughtered them in the desert.' (Ex 14:15-16).
- Because of God's promises to the patriarchs: "Remember your servants Abraham, Isaac and Israel, to whom you swore by your own self: 'I will make your descendants as numerous as the stars in the sky and I will give your descendants all this land I promised them, and it will be their inheritance forever'" (Ex 32:13).
- Because of God's merciful character: "Now may the Lord's strength be displayed, just as you have declared: 'The Lord is slow to anger, abounding in love and forgiving sin and rebellion. Yet he does not leave the guilty unpunished; he punishes the children for the sin of the fathers to the third and fourth generation.' In accordance with your great love, forgive the sin of these people..." (Ex14:17-19).
- Because of God's precedent: "... Just as you have pardoned them from the time they left Egypt until now" (Ex1.4:19)

Application:

We need to imitate Moses in our intercessory prayers. We need to appeal to God based on His promises, character, righteousness, and precedents. When we learn to pray like Moses, we will know how to pray according to God's will.

Hannah's Prayers
1 Samuel 1:10-11

During the time when judges ruled, Israel had no king. Everyone did what he thought was right, and each generation became worse than the previous one.

Elkanah had two wives; one named Hannah and the other Peninnah. Peninnah had children, but Hannah had no children.

Every year Elkanah left his home in Ramah and went to Shiloh to worship and sacrifice to the Lord Almighty. Shiloh was where Eli and his two sons served as priests.

Each year, Elkanah gave portions of the sacrificial meat to his wife Peninnah and to all her children. But Elkanah gave Hannah a double portion because he loved her and because the Lord had made Hannah unable to have children. Peninnah kept provoking Hannah, never letting her forget that she had no children. Every time Hannah went up to the house of the Lord, her rival provoked her until she cried and wouldn't eat.

Her husband Elkanah asked her, "Hannah, why are you crying? Why don't you eat? Why are you depressed? Don't I mean more to you than ten sons?" (1 Sam 1:1-8).

Once after they had eaten their meal in Shiloh, Hannah slipped away and entered the tabernacle. Priest Eli was sitting on a chair by the entrance to the Lord's tabernacle. Hannah cried and cried in bitterness of soul. Hannah prayed to the Lord. Hannah made a promise, "Oh, Lord Almighty, if you'll only look at my misery and remember me by giving me a son, I'll give him back to you all the days of his life. No one will ever use a razor to cut his hair."

Hannah kept praying to the Lord. Priest Eli watched her mouth. Hannah prayed in her heart silently; her lips moved, but no words were heard. (*Israelites usually prayed aloud; feast days often became occasions for heavy drinking. See Isaiah 22:13 and Amos 2:8.*) Eli thought, "She's drunk," and said to Hannah, "You're drunk! How long will you keep on getting drunk? Throw away your wine!"

Hannah replied, "Oh, no, sir. I'm a woman who is deeply troubled. I haven't been drinking wine nor beer; I poured out my soul to the Lord. I've been praying because of my desperate torment and sorrow."

Eli answered, "Go in peace. And may the God of Israel give you what you've asked of him."

Then Hannah ate something, and she was dejected no longer (1 Sam 1:9-18).

Elkanah's family returned home to Ramah. Hannah became pregnant and gave birth to a son. She named him Samuel, saying, "I asked the Lord for him" (1 Sam 1:19-20).

Hannah stayed at home and nursed her son until she weaned him. Shortly after weaning Samuel, Elkanah and Hannah took him to the tabernacle of the Lord at Shiloh. Hannah presented the little child to Eli, and told him, "Sir, I'm the woman who stood at this very spot praying to the Lord. I prayed for this child, and the Lord gave me what I asked for. Now I give him back to the Lord. He's dedicated to God for all his life" (1 Sam 1:21-28).

Commentary:

Samuel's history began before he was born; it began with his mother's prayer asking for a son.

Hannah felt bitterness of soul, great anguish, and resentfulness. Hannah took those bitter and resentful feelings to God honestly in prayer (1 Sam 1:10).

Hannah began her prayer by calling on the Lord Almighty (1 Sam 1:11). That title has the idea of "Lord of the Mighty Armies." Hannah felt attacked by her rival, so she called on the Lord of the Mighty Armies to be her protector.

Hannah promised God that if He answered her prayer and gave her a son, she would give her son to the work of the Lord. She vowed he would be a Nazirite from birth (1 Sam 1:11). According to Numbers 6, the vow of a Nazirite included the following:
- Abstinence from any product from a grape vine (*signifying distance from fleshly pleasures*).
- Not to mourn for the dead, nor to come near a dead body (*death shows the corruption and the fruit of sin; this also showed that the Nazirite had greater concerns than the ordinary joys and sorrows of life*).
- Never cutting the hair (*this was a public, visible sign to others of the vow*).

Hannah continued to pray (1 Sam 1:12). She prayed for a long time. The Bible only recorded a summary of Hannah's prayer.

Hannah prayed from her heart; her lips moved, but her voice was silent (1 Sam 1:13).

Hannah received baby Samuel as an answer to prayer, and she gave him up to God according to her vow (1 Sam 1:26-28).

Application:
When we feel bitterness, misery, and resentment, our reaction should be to pray and honestly talk to God about the things that give us those feelings.

Effective prayer can be silent. Praying aloud can help us focus our thoughts, yet Hannah's prayer shows us that valid prayer doesn't need to be vocal.

Promises made to God in prayer should be kept.

1 Samuel 2:1-10
When Hannah took her son Samuel to priest Eli, Hannah sang a song praising the Lord (1 Sam 2:1-10).

"Then Hannah prayed and said: 'My heart rejoices in the Lord; in the Lord my horn is lifted high. My mouth boasts over my enemies, for I delight in your deliverance. There is no one holy like the Lord; there is no one besides you; there is no Rock like our God' (1 Sam 2:1-2 NIV).

Commentary:
Hannah used poetic language to celebrate Samuel's birth and to express her praise to God who answered her prayer (1 Sam 2:1-10).

Application:
When God answers our prayers, we need to respond to God with praise and thanksgiving.

Jabez's Prayer 1 Chronicles 4:10
"Jabez cried out to the God of Israel, 'Oh, that you would bless me and enlarge my territory! Let your hand be with me, and keep me from harm so that I will be free from pain.' And God granted his request" (1 Chr 4:10 NIV).

Commentary:
Jabez's mother named her baby boy, Jabez, which means "Painful" because his birth was painful to her. Jabez's birth brought sorrow, but Jabez became an honorable man (1 Chr 4:9).

Jabez is mentioned in 1 Chronicles 2:55 as a location where scribes' families lived. Jabez either founded a school for scribes, or other scribes respected him so much that they moved to live close to him.

Observations about Jabez's prayer:
- Jabez addressed his prayer to the covenant God, the God of Israel.
- Jabez petitioned for God's blessings. To ask for God's blessing is to request Him to bestow divine privileges and protection.
- Jabez petitioned for prosperity: "Enlarge my territory." It is clear that Jabez asked for enlargement of means or authority or land or influence. Since he probably founded a school for scribes (1 Chr 2:55), he was probably requesting an enlargement of his influence.
- Jabez petitioned for God's presence: "That your hand be with me," was a prayer for strength, protection, and guidance.
- Jabez petitioned for protection and purity: "Keep me from harm."
- Jabez petitioned for freedom from pain: The name Jabez implied "Pain"; however, Jabez requested that he neither experience nor cause pain.

Observation about the answer to Jabez's prayer:
- "God granted Jabez's petitions. God heard and answered the request of this honorable man.

Application:
God hears and responds to the prayers of His people. God may not always give us what we ask for in exactly the way that we ask, but He hears and answers people who pray.

Psalmist David's Prayers
Psalm 19:12-14

"But who can discern their own errors? Forgive my hidden faults. Keep your servant also from willful sins; may they not rule over me. Then I will be blameless, innocent of great transgression. May the words of my mouth and the meditation of my heart be pleasing in your sight, O Lord, my Rock and my Redeemer" (Psa 19:12-14 NIV).

Commentary:

Psalmist David prayed that:
- God would forgive him of his hidden faults. He wanted God to forgive him for wrong-doings that were hidden from himself and others. He wanted forgiveness from things that David didn't think were wrong, but God condemned them as wrong.
- God would keep him from intentional sinful actions (Psa 19:13). He prayed for God to help him avoid doing things that he knew were wrong. He wanted God to protect him from strong desires that would push him to do wrong regardless of the consequences.
- God would govern his speech and thoughts. "Words of my mouth," refers to speech in common conversation. "Meditation of my heart" refers to the thoughts of his heart, his inward thoughts that continually revolve in his mind. David prayed that both his spoken words and his silent thoughts might be pleasing in God's sight.

Application:

We are possessed with a sinful nature and a corrupt heart. Therefore, we may consider that some of our thoughts, words, or actions are proper; however, God may condemn them as sin. We may be guilty of wrong-doing before God, and we are not even aware that we have sinned.

We may know that something is wrong, but we want to do it so badly that we intentionally act on our desires regardless of the consequences. We are tempted to think lustful thoughts, to say cruel words, or do things to intentionally hurt others. We know they are wrong, but we still want to do them.

It is clear that our spoken words and our thoughts have the capacity to please or displease God. We need to pray that both our spoken words and silent thoughts are pleasing to God.

Psalm 25:1-7

"In you, Lord my God, I put my trust. I trust in you; do not let me be put to shame, nor let my enemies triumph over me. No one who hopes in you will ever be put to shame, but shame will come on those who are treacherous without cause. Show me your ways, Lord, teach me your paths. Guide me in your truth and teach me, for you are God my Savior, and my hope is in you all day long. Remember, Lord, your great mercy and love, for they are from of old. Do not remember the sins of my youth and my rebellious ways; according to your love remember me, for you, Lord, are good." (Psa 25:1-7 NIV).

Commentary:

In his prayer, the psalmist David made affirmations and requests:
- David's affirmations:
  - His trust was in the Lord his God (Psa 25:1).
  - Shame does not come to people who hope in God; it comes to the unfaithful (Psa 25:3).
  - God was his Savior (Psa 25:5).
  - God's compassionate and merciful deeds exist from eternity (Psa 25:6).
- David's request:
  - Not be put to shame (Psa 25:2).
  - For his enemies not to triumph over him (Psa 25:2).
  - To be taught God's ways (Psa 25:4).
  - For God to lead him and teach him truth (Psa 25:5).
  - For God to forgive and forget his youthful wrong-doings and his rebellious ways (Psa 24:7).

Application:

We also need to pray for God to forgive and forget our sins, to be our guide, and for help against enemies who oppose us as we do God's will.

Psalm 51:1-17

"Have mercy on me, O God, according to your unfailing love; according to your great compassion blot out my transgressions. Wash away all my iniquity and cleanse me from my sin. For I know my transgressions, and my sin is always before me. Against you, you only, have I sinned and done what is evil in your sight; so you are right in your verdict and justified when you judge. Surely I was sinful at birth, sinful from the time my mother conceived me. Yet you desired faithfulness even in the womb; you taught me wisdom in that secret place. Cleanse me with hyssop, and I will be clean; wash me, and I will be whiter than snow. Let me hear joy and gladness; let the bones you have crushed rejoice. Hide your face from my sins and blot out all my iniquity. Create in me a pure heart, O God, and renew a steadfast spirit within me. Do not cast me from your presence or take your Holy Spirit from me. Restore to me the joy of your salvation and grant me a willing spirit, to sustain me. Then I will teach transgressors your ways, so that sinners will turn back to you. Deliver me from the guilt of bloodshed, O God, you who are God my Savior, and my tongue will sing of your righteousness. Open my lips, Lord, and my mouth will declare your praise. You do not delight in sacrifice, or I would bring it; you do not take pleasure in burnt offerings. My sacrifice, O God, is a broken spirit; a broken and contrite heart you, God, will not despise" (Psa 51:1-17 NIV).

Commentary:

King David wrote this psalm after the prophet Nathan confronted him for his adultery with Bathsheba. From the roof of his palace, King David saw the woman Bathsheba bathing. She was the wife of Uriah, a soldier who was fighting in David's army. King David sent his servants to bring Bathsheba to his palace, and they had sex. Later Bathsheba sent word to David that she was going to have his baby. So King David brought the soldier Uriah home. David tried to make Uriah go home so he would have sex with Bathsheba and would think that the baby was his. Uriah refused to go home, so David sent Uriah to a dangerous post in the war. Uriah was killed in battle. Then David married Bathsheba. God sent the prophet Nathan to confront David about his sin (2 Sam 11:1 - 12:15).

Psalm 51 is the record of David's repentance for his sin in the matter of Uriah. In this psalm, David:

- Confesses his sin (Psa 51:3-6).
- Prayed earnestly for the forgiveness of his sin (Psa 51:1, 2, 7, 9).
- Prayed for restoration of joy (Psa 51:8, 12).
- Prayed for restoration of a relationship with God (Psa 51:10, 11, 14).
- Prayed for the ability to tell others about God (Psa:51:15).
- Promised to try to turn other sinners to God (Psa 51:13).
- Recognized that the sacrifice that pleases God is a broken spirit (Psa 51:16-17).

Application:

It is not innocence which makes a person good in God's sight. Rather, the guilty sinner becomes right with God when he:
- Considers his sin repugnant.
- Trusts in God's mercy for forgiveness.
- Struggles with God's help to reconstruct his life to serve God.

The person guilty of wrong-doing needs to:
- Confess his sin.
- Ask God for forgiveness.
- Trust God to show him mercy.
- Make a commitment to serve God.

Psalm 139:23-24

"Search me, God, and know my heart; test me and know my anxious thoughts. See if there is any offensive way in me, and lead me in the way everlasting" (Psa 139:23-24 NIV).

Commentary:

David began Psalm 139 with the contemplation of God's omniscience when he stated that a characteristic of God is that He searches the heart; that God had examined him, and that God knew him (Psalm 139:1).

David's prayer made four requests to God (Psa 139:23-24):
- <u>For God to search his heart</u> (Psa 139:23). David wanted God to examine him with the closest scrutiny, not that God would know him, but that David would know himself. This request indicated David's self-distrust and desire to be free from self-deception.

- <u>For God to test his thoughts</u> (Psa 139:23). David wanted God to examine not only his outward conduct, but his inner thoughts. He wanted God to examine what passed through his mind, what occupied his imagination and his memory, what secured his affections, and what controlled his will. David wanted God to test him and refine him — to do what must be done to ensure he had pure thoughts. David wanted God to test his thoughts similar to the way metals are tried and tested by the fiery furnace. Faith, like gold, is more precious when tried by fire. David would willingly submit to any discipline, undesirable situation, or fiery testing that would enable the true character of his thoughts to be made clear to himself.
- <u>For God to examine his actions</u>. David wanted to cast out actions that were offensive to God. David wanted to know if he was doing anything that was harmful to God. He wanted God to make sure he was not on the road to ruin. He wanted to do God's will instead of getting in God's way.
- <u>For guidance in "the way everlasting.</u>" David knew that he had a sinful human nature and that he was inclined to do evil. He knew that it would take God's Spirit to lead him in the paths of righteousness. David's desire went beyond guidance for temporary situations; he wanted guidance for "the way everlasting."

Application:

If our greatest desire is to stand approved in the sight of God, we will pray psalmist David's prayer. We need a desire to be saved from self-deception and guided in the way of true life. The Christian who wants to be free from self-deception and overcome his own shortcomings in order to become more acceptable in God's sight will have the desire for God to put him to the test. If we would please God, both divine searching and divine guidance are indispensable for us.

I confess, it's easier for me to pray Jabez's prayer that I may be free from pain (1 Chr 4:10) than to pray David's prayer for God to put me to the test (Psa 139:23). If I were more concerned for my character than my comfort, I would welcome God's testing.

Solomon's Prayer 1 Kings 3:9
"So give your servant a discerning heart to govern your people and to distinguish between right and wrong. For who is able to govern this great people of yours?" (1 Ki 3:9 NIV).

Commentary:
Solomon went to Gibeon to offer sacrifices to God. The Lord asked Solomon in a dream, "What do you want me to give you?"

Solomon requested a discerning heart.

The Lord was delighted with Solomon's request, and promised Solomon, "You've asked for wisdom and not for a long life, nor riches, nor the death of your enemies. I'll give you what you requested. I'll give you wisdom and an understanding heart. I'll also give you what you didn't request: riches and honor. And if you follow me and obey my laws and commands, I'll give you a long life" (1 Kin 3:4-15; 1 Chr 1:2-12).

Solomon prayed for a discerning or an understanding heart so he could govern God's people. Solomon was king and people would bring to him controversies or causes for him to resolve. He wanted to discern between good and bad so that he would not give wrong punishment as a result of prejudice or passion or personal preference. This would protect him from giving wrong sentences, and calling evil good, or good evil.

Solomon recognized his limitations when he confessed "I am only a little child and don't know how to carry out my duties" (1 Ki 3:7 NIV). Solomon had become a man. He must have been at least twenty years old, but he was raw and inexperienced in matters of government.

Application:
We need to be aware of our limitations. Self-confidence results in self-deception. Self-awareness of our own limitations should result in our seeking understanding from God to do the work He wants us to do. God gives unqualified people responsibility. Then God enables those unqualified individuals, who depend on Him, to do a divine task.

Asa's Prayer 2 Chronicles 14:11
"Then Asa called to the Lord his God and said, 'Lord there is no one like you to help the powerless against the mighty. Help us, Lord

our God, for we rely on you, and in your name we have come against this vast army. Lord you are our God; do not let mere mortals prevail against you'" (2 Chr 14:11 NIV).

Commentary:
Asa was the great-grandson of King Solomon. Asa became king of Judah (1 Kin 15:1-8). King Asa did what was right in the eyes of the Lord, as his ancestor David had done. King Asa expelled the male shrine prostitutes from the land and got rid of all the idols made by his predecessors. Asa's grandmother had made a memorial to the whore-goddess Asherah. Therefore, Asa removed his grandmother from her position as queen mother. Asa's heart was committed to the Lord (1 Kin 15:11-15). King Asa commanded Judah to seek the Lord, the God of their ancestors, and to obey His commands (2 Chr 14:4).

King Asa had an army of 580,000 fighting men. Zerah from Sudan came with a million fighting men to attack Asa. Asa called on the Lord his God. The Lord attacked the Sudanese army, and the Sudanese army fled (2 Chr 14:9-12).

Application:
King Asa's prayer contains the essence of what ought to be the Christian response in reference to threatening dangers and conflicts of life:
- Do what is right in the eyes of God at all times. King Asa himself did right in the eyes of the Lord (1 Kin 15:11-15) and he sought to lead others to obey God (2 Chr 14:9-12).
- Fulfill one's own responsibility. King Asa set his troops in order and took his army to confront the enemy.
- Be aware of one's own powerlessness. Asa's army was outnumbered two to one. Self-distrust and helplessness are conditions for God to give victory. Our consciousness of our need is our opening the door for God to come in.
- Recognize one's inability and trust in God's ability. Asa realized that God enables people with no power to face the powerful. Only God can enable the weak to confront the mighty. The minority who depend on God have the advantage over the majority who oppose God.
- Self-distrust and trust in God leads to courageous advance. King Asa was aware of his army's weakness and

the enemies' strength, but he put his trust in God and advanced to battle.
- Experience victory by recognizing God as our God and making God's cause our cause. Asa confessed, "Lord you are our God; do not let mere mortals prevail against you." If God is our God and if God's causes are our causes, we will share in His victories.

Elijah's Prayer 1 Kings 18:20-40; James 5:17-18

Elijah prayed for it not to rain, and it did not rain for three and a half years. Again Elijah prayed for rain, and it rained (Ja 5:17-18).

God miraculously answered Elijah's prayer on Mt. Carmel when he rained fire from heaven in the showdown between God and the false god Baal (1 Ki 18:20-40, especially 37-38).

Back-story:

King Ahab of Israel did worse than all the kings before him. Ahab did more to provoke the Lord God to anger than all the previous kings of Israel (1 Kin 16:29-33).

Prophet Elijah confronted Ahab and prophesied that the Lord God would send a severe drought for several years (1 Kin 17:1-16).

Three years after Prophet Elijah prophesied the drought, the Lord told Elijah, "Present yourself to Ahab, and I will send rain on the land."

Elijah told King Ahab, "Gather everyone in Israel at Mount Carmel. Bring the prophets who eat at Jezebel's table, the 450 prophets of Baal and the 400 prophets of the prostitute goddess Asherah" (1 Kin 18:1-19).

Ahab summoned everyone in Israel, especially the prophets, to Mount Carmel. Elijah challenged the people, "How long will you try to serve both Baal and the Lord? If the Lord is God, follow him; but if Baal is God, follow him."

Nobody said a word.

Elijah spoke, "Get two bulls. Let Baal's 450 prophets butcher one bull and lay it on the wood, but not set fire to it. I'll prepare the other bull and put it on the wood, but not set fire to it. Then you pray to your god, and I'll pray to the Lord. The god who answers by fire, he's the real God."

The people agreed, "You have a good plan; do it!"

Baal's prophets took one of the bulls, prepared it, and called on Baal. Baal's prophets tried every religious trick they knew until the time for the evening sacrifice. But nothing happened.

Then Elijah took twelve stones to build an altar in honor of the Lord. Elijah dug a ditch around it. Elijah arranged the wood, butchered the bull and laid it on the wood as a sacrifice offering. Then Elijah ordered, "Fill four large jars with water and drench both the offering and the wood." Then he said, "Do it again," and they did it a second time. Then Elijah said, "Do it a third time," and they did it a third time. Water ran down around the altar and filled the ditch.

Elijah stepped near the altar and prayed, "O Lord, God of Abraham, Isaac and Israel, make known to these people that you, O Lord, are God, and that you are giving these people another chance to turn their hearts back to you."

Immediately fire from the Lord fell and burned up the sacrifice offering, the wood, the stones, the soil, and even the water in the ditch.

The people bowed down to the ground and shouted, "The Lord, he is God! The Lord, he is God!"

Elijah commanded, "Seize the prophets of Baal!" The people seized them, and Elijah slaughtered the prophets of Baal (1 Kin 18:20-40).

Elijah prayed. Then Elijah ordered King Ahab, "Hitch up your chariot and get down from the mountain before heavy rain delays you."

A heavy rain fell and Ahab rode off to Jezreel. The Lord's power enabled Elijah to run ahead of Ahab's chariot until they reached Jezreel (1 Kin 18:41-46).

Commentary:

The Lord God is the only true God with power to act. The competition between Baal's prophets and Elijah on Mount Carmel was not to decide whether the Lord or Baal was more powerful. It was to determine which was the only true God. Elijah's word (1 Kin 18:22-25), his prayer (1 Kin 18:37), and the acclamation of the people (1 Kin 18:39) show that it was a battle to determine who was the only true God.

Application:
There is only one true God, and He is Jehovah, the Lord God. He is the only God who answers prayers.

Jonah's Prayer Jonah 2:1-10

From inside the fish, Jonah prayed to the Lord his God. He said: "In my distress I called to the Lord, and he answered me. From deep in the realm of the dead, I called for help, and you listened to my cry. You hurled me into the depths, into the very heart of the seas, and the currents swirled about me; all your waves and breakers swept over me. I said, 'I have been banished from your sight; yet I will look again toward your holy temple.'

"The engulfing waters threatened me, the deep surrounded me; seaweed was wrapped around my head. To the roots of the mountains I sank down; the earth beneath barred me in forever. But you, Lord my God, brought my life up from the pit. When my life was ebbing away, I remembered you, Lord, and my prayer rose to you, to your holy temple. Those who cling to worthless idols turn away from God's love for them. But I, with shouts of grateful praise; I will sacrifice to you. What I have vowed I will make good. I will say, 'Salvation comes from the Lord.' And the Lord commanded the fish, and it vomited Jonah onto dry land" (Jon 2:1-10).

Back-story:
The Lord told Jonah to go to the city of Nineveh and preach against it (Jon 1:1-2). Nineveh was the capital city of Assyria, the greatest enemy of the nation of Israel.

However, Jonah found a ship bound for Tarshish which was the opposite direction from Nineveh (Jon 1:3).

Then the Lord created a violent storm. The sailors threw the cargo overboard to lighten the ship. Meanwhile, Jonah had gone below deck into the hold of the ship and he fell into a deep sleep. The captain found Jonah and said, "How can you sleep? Get up and pray to your god! Maybe your god will notice our desperate situation and rescue us."

The sailors drew straws to find out who was the culprit on the ship responsible for the storm. Jonah got the short straw and he confessed that he was running away from the Lord. Jonah told the sailors, "Get rid of me, and you'll get rid of the storm."

The men took Jonah and threw him overboard. Immediately the raging sea grew calm (Jon 1:4-16). The Lord provided a large fish to swallow Jonah. Jonah was inside the stomach of the fish for three days and three nights (Jon 1:17).

Jonah prayed to the Lord his God (Jon 2:1-9). The Lord spoke to the fish and it vomited Jonah out of its stomach onto dry land (Jon 2:10).

Commentary:

Jonah was inside the fish's belly, and he prayed to the Lord his God. Jonah had been a praying man, and a prophet of the Lord. The Bible story implies that Jonah did not pray while he was disobeying the will of God while he was going to Joppa. Some observations about Jonah's prayer:
- When he prayed: when he was in trouble.
- Where he prayed: in the fish's belly.
- To whom he prayed: to the Lord his God.
- What he prayed: a prayer of thanksgiving for his rescue from death by drowning. He thanked God for saving him from a deserved punishment even though his circumstances in the fish's belly were undesirable.

Application:

The person who is running from God will neglect praying to God.

We need to pray when we are in affliction because we have been trying to run from God.

Any place can become a place for prayer.

King Hezekiah's Prayer of Deliverance from Enemies 2 Kings 19:15-19

"And Hezekiah prayed to the Lord; 'Lord the God of Israel, enthroned between the cherubim, you alone are God over all the kingdoms of the earth. You have made heaven and earth. Give ear, Lord, and hear; open your eyes, Lord, and see; listen to the words Sennacherib has sent to ridicule the living God. It is true, Lord, that the Assyrian kings have laid waste these nations and their lands. They have thrown their gods into the fire and destroyed them, for they were not gods, but only wood and stone, fashioned by human hands. Now, Lord, our God, deliver us from his hand, so that all the kingdoms of the earth may know that you alone, Lord, are God" (2 Kin 19:15-19)

Back-story:
Hezekiah was 25 years old when he became king of Judah. He did what was right in the eyes of the Lord. He obeyed the commands the Lord had given Moses. The Lord was with him; he had success in everything he did (2 Kg 18:1-8).

In King Hezekiah's fourth year, Shalmaneser, king of Assyria, attacked Samaria, and after three years captured it. Samaria was captured because the Israelites had not obeyed the Lord their God (2 Kg 18:9-12).

The king of Assyria sent his top three military chiefs to King Hezekiah in Jerusalem. The Assyrian field commander shouted a message for King Hezekiah, "Hear the word of the great king of Assyria! Do not let Hezekiah fool you. Do not let Hezekiah persuade you to trust in the Lord. The king of Assyria says, Make peace with me. Then I will take you to a land of grain and new wine, a land of bread and vineyards, a land of olive trees and honey. Choose life and not death! Do not listen to Hezekiah's lies when he says, `The Lord will deliver us.' The Lord cannot deliver Jerusalem from me!" (2 Kg 18:26-35; Is 36:1-20).

Sennacherib received a report that the king of Egypt was marching out to fight against him. He sent a letter to Hezekiah, "Do not let the god you depend on deceive you when he says, `Jerusalem will not fall to the king of Assyria.' The kings of Assyria have destroyed country after country. The gods of those people did not deliver them?" (2 Kg 19:9-13; Is 37:8-13).

Hezekiah read the letter. Then he went up to the temple of the Lord and spread it out before the Lord. Hezekiah prayed.

Commentary:
Prayer was King Hezekiah's first response to a crisis. Hezekiah received the letter from the Assyrian king with its threats, and he took the problem before God in prayer (2 Kg 19:14-19). Prayer should seek the glory of God above everything else. Hezekiah's prayer (2 Kg 19:14-19; Is 37:15-16) did not just ask for the deliverance from the Assyrians, he pleaded for God's name to be glorified (2 Kg 19:19).

Application:
Prayer should be our first response in a crisis, and as we pray, we should take our problem to God.

Our primary concern in prayer should be that God be glorified.

Habakkuk's Prayer Habakkuk 3:17-18

"Though the fig tree does not bud and there are no grapes on the vines, though the olive crop fails and the fields produce no food, though there are no sheep in the pen and no cattle in the stalls, yet I will rejoice in the Lord, I will be joyful in God my Savior" (Hab 3:17-18 NIV).

Back-story:
The book of Habakkuk opens with the prophet's complaint to God (Hab 1:2, 3, 4). The situation in Judah was chaotic with anarchy, riots, and corrupt judges. The laws were not obeyed, and no justice existed. Habakkuk complained that, worst of all, God was doing nothing about it. God answered the prophet Habakkuk by saying He was working, but the prophet wouldn't believe what He was going to do. God was going to use the Babylonians (Chaldeans) as an instrument of judgment (Hab 1:5-11). Habakkuk questioned God because the Babylonians were worse than the citizens of Judah (Hab 1:12-17). Most of chapter three consists of Habakkuk looking back at the great acts of God in the past: God overcame the Egyptians at the Red Sea; God brought the Israelites through the experiences of the desert and into the Promised Land; God overthrew the nations of Canaan and planted his people in the Promised Land (Hab 3:1-5). But at the present time, Habakkuk trembled with fear expecting the day of trouble (Hab 3:16). Habakkuk imagined the worst-case scenario that could happen (Hab 3:17). But even if the worse-case scenario happened, Habakkuk said he would still rejoice in the Lord and find joy in the God of his salvation (Hab 3:18).

Application:
We too need the commitment that when God answers our prayers in ways that are undesirable to us, and even if we experience the worst-case scenario, we will still rejoice in the Lord and find joy in the God of our salvation. Our commitment to God is

not dependent on God blessing us or answering our prayers the way we request.

Nehemiah's Prayer Nehemiah 9:5-38
　Nehemiah's prayer reviewed God's historic action:
- God as creator (Neh 9:6 // Gen 1-11)
- God's choice of Abraham (Neh 9:7-8 // Gen 12-50)
- God's actions in the Exodus (Neh 9:9-14 // Book of Exodus)
- God's faithful care and provision during the wilderness wandering period (Neh 9:15-21 // Book of Numbers)
- God's promises to Abraham fulfilled (Neh 9:22-25 // Book of Joshua)
- Israel's further rebellion (Neh 9:20-31 // time of the Judges)
- God's covenant faithfulness and Israel's unfaithfulness continued (Neh 9:32-38 // the time of the Monarchy)

Commentary:
　Nehemiah, chapter nine, records the longest prayer in the Bible. The prayer shows the theological basis of Israel's history: God's faithfulness to His covenant; Israel's unfaithfulness to God's covenant. It was not God's powerlessness, but Israel's sin that brought destruction and exile; however, it was God's character and power that enabled Israel to exist and return to the Promised Land.

Application:
　Our prayers should refer to life-lessons we learn from Bible stories.

Mary's Prayer Luke 1:46-55
　"And Mary said: 'My soul glorifies the Lord and my spirit rejoices in God my Savior, for he has been mindful of the humble state of his servant. From now on all generations will call me blessed, for the Mighty One has done great things for me – holy is his name. His mercy extends to those who fear him, from generation to generation. He has performed mighty deeds with his arm; he has scattered those who are proud in their inmost thoughts. He has brought down rulers from their thrones but has lifted up the humble. He has filled the hungry with good things but has sent the

rich away empty. He has helped his servant Israel, remembering to be merciful to Abraham and his descendants forever, just as he promised our ancestors'" (Lk 1:46-55 NIV).

Commentary:
Mary's prayer was a song of praise that expressed:
- Personal praise to God for His treatment of her. Mary recognized her humble state as God's servant, and she recognized God as Sovereign Master. Mary addressed God as the Mighty One who is also her Savior. Mary recognized, that despite her humble position, she will be honored by all generations because God the Almighty has done great things on her behalf.
- Expanded praise to include all who fear God. God's mercy extends to those who fear Him. The blessings of Luke 1:50-53 are for the needy; however, they are only for the poor and hungry who look to God for care.
- Recognition that God shows His strength by upsetting social structures; God dethrones rulers, and humbles the mighty.

Applications:
- God is worthy of praise for how He blesses insignificant individuals and for how He takes care of His own.
- Understanding God's blessing moves believers to joy and praise because the Almighty cares personally for us and acts on our behalf.
- God owes us nothing; we owe God everything. All the good things that come from God are acts of grace.
- God deserves our praise because His redemptive work begins here on earth. God fills the needy with both hope and food.
- Mary becomes an example of a simple, poor, peasant girl who was touched by divine power and presence.

The Leper's Prayer Matthew 8:2-3
A man with leprosy came and knelt before Jesus and said, "Lord, if you are willing, you can make me clean." Jesus extended his hand, touched the man and said, "I am willing, be clean!" Immediately the man was cleansed of his leprosy (Mat 8:2-3).

Commentary:

In the ancient world, leprosy was a terrible, destructive disease. The leper had no hope of improvement. The leper came to Jesus with a sense of need and desperation. The leper worshiped Jesus by kneeling before Him. The leper knew that Jesus had the ability to heal. His only question was if Jesus was willing to heal him. Jesus touched the man and immediately his leprosy was cleansed. The former leper's life was changed forever. He was not only healed, but as he requested, he was cleansed.

Application:

We need to worship Jesus for who He is and not for what we want Him to do for us. We need to recognize His power to answer our prayer request, but still recognize that He has the right to say "Yes" or "No" to our request.

I watched as my wife's health deteriorated at a fast pace during her last year. Each health crisis was harder for her and increased her suffering. I struggled with keeping faith in what Jesus was able to do and accepting what He was willing to do for my wife.

Tax Collector's Prayer Luke 18:13

"But the tax collector stood at a distance. He would not even look up to heaven, but beat his breast and said, 'God, have mercy on me, a sinner'" (Lk 18:13 NIV).

Back-story:

Jesus told the following parable to some who were sure that they were upright but despised everyone else, "Two men went up to the temple to pray. One was a Pharisee and the other a tax collector. The Pharisee stood in front of everyone and prayed about himself, 'God, I thank you that I'm not like other people. I'm not a robber. I'm not an evildoer. I haven't committed adultery. I'm definitely not like this tax collector. I fast twice a week and tithe on all my income.'

"However, the tax collector stood a distance from the people. He wouldn't even look up to heaven. Instead he beat his breast and said, 'God, have mercy on me, a sinner.'

"I tell you that the tax collector, rather than the Pharisee, went home justified, being approved by God. For everyone who honors himself will be humbled, and he who humbles himself will be honored" (Lk 18:9-14).

Commentary:
Sinners are not justified by the good they do, but by acknowledging their sins and calling on God for forgiveness. The tax collector was not justified by obeying the Old Testament Law, but by his repentance, his humble approach to God, his acknowledgment of sin, and his faith in God.

The person who is full of himself when he prays will not have his prayer heard by God. The Pharisee went up to the temple to pray, but was full of himself and his own goodness. God did not accept him nor his prayer.

Applications:
Our sins are forgiven when we acknowledge them and call on God for forgiveness.

If we are self-confident, our prayers will not be heard by God.

Jesus' Prayers

Jesus' Prayer Before Resurrecting Lazarus John 11:42
"Then Jesus looked up and said, 'Father, I thank you that you have heard me. I knew that you always hear me, but I said this for the benefit of the people standing here, that they may believe that you sent me.'" (Jn 11:41-42 NIV).

Commentary:
It appears that Jesus had prayed when He heard of Lazarus' sickness. At that time Jesus stated that Lazarus' sickness was not unto death, but for the glory of God and that the Son of God might be glorified (Jn 11:4). Jesus addressed the Father before those unbelieving Jews, that they might see that it was by God's power that He was going to perform the miracle of bringing Lazarus back to life. And Jesus offered a prayer of thanksgiving, for the Father's answer to this and all his petitions.

Jesus addressed His prayer to the Father but He also intended for the audience to be informed by the prayer.

Application:
The main purpose of prayer is to talk to God the Father; however, public prayer can legitimately be used as an educational tool.

Jesus' High Priestly Prayer John 17
After Jesus said this, He looked toward heaven and prayed: "Father, the hour has come. Glorify your Son, that your Son may glorify you. For you granted him authority over all people that he might give eternal life to all those you have given him. Now this is eternal life: that they know you, the only true God, and Jesus Christ, whom you have sent. I have brought you glory on earth by finishing the work you gave me to do. And now, Father, glorify me in your presence with the glory I had with you before the world began.

"I have revealed you to those whom you gave me out of the world. They were yours; you gave them to me and they have obeyed your word. Now they know that everything you have given me comes from you. For I gave them the words you gave me and they accepted them. They knew with a certainty that I came from you, and they believed that you sent me. I pray for them. I am not praying for the world, but for those you have given me, for they are yours. All I have is yours, and all you have is mine. And glory has come to me through them. I will remain in the world no longer, but they are still in the world, and I am coming to you. Holy Father, protect them by the power of your name, the name you gave me, so that they may be one as we are one. While I was with them, I protected them and kept them safe by that name you gave me. None has been lost except the one doomed to destruction so that Scripture would be fulfilled.

"I am coming to you now, but I say these things while I am still in the world, so that they may have the full measure of my joy within them. I have given them your word and the world has hated them, for they are not of the world any more than I am of the world. My prayer is not that you take them out of the world but that you protect them from the evil one. They are not of the world, even as I am not of it. Sanctify them by the truth; your word is truth. As you sent me into the world, I have sent them into the world. For them I sanctify myself, that they too may be truly sanctified.

"My prayer is not for them alone. I pray also for those who will believe in me through their message, that all of them may be one,

Father, just as you are in me and I am in you. May they also be in us so that the world may believe that you have sent me. I have given them the glory that you gave me, that they may be one as we are one – I in them and you in me – so that they may be brought to complete unity. Then the world will know that you sent me and have loved them even as you have loved me.

"Father, I want those you have given me to be with me where I am, and to see my glory, the glory you have given me because you loved me before the creation of the world.

"Righteous Father, though the world does not know you, I know you, and they know that you have sent me. I have made you known to them, and will continue to make you known in order that the love you have for me may be in them and that I myself may be in them" (Jn 17:1-26).

Commentary:

John 17 is the only long, continuous prayer of Jesus that is recorded in the Gospels.

There are four parts of Jesus' prayer:

1st **Jesus prayed for himself** (Jn 17:1-5)
- Factual information: "Father, the hour has come" (Jn 17:1). The time for Jesus' death, burial, resurrection, and ascension had arrived.
- 1st Petition: "Glorify your Son, that your Son may glorify you" (Jn 17:1). The ultimate goal of Jesus' petition was to glorify the Father.
- Explanation of how Jesus' glorification will glorify the Father (Jn 17:2-3). The Father had given the Son authority and power in order that the Son's crucifixion might give eternal life to people (Jn 17:2).
- Eternal life defined: people knowing God the Father and Jesus (Jn 17:3).
- Rationale for Jesus' second petition: Jesus had accomplished the work the Father gave Him to do (Jn 17:4).
- 2nd Petition: For the Father to immediately give Jesus the glory he had with the Father before the world began (Jn 17:5).

2nd **Jesus interceded on behalf of His immediate disciples** (Jn 17:6-19)
- Report: Jesus identified the disciples' relationship to the Father ("they were yours") and to the son ("you gave them to me") (Jn 17:6). He reported on what they did with His teaching – "they have obeyed your word" (Jn 17:6), they knew all things which the Father had given to Jesus (Jn 17:7), they knew that Jesus came from the Father (Jn 17:7), and they believed that the Father sent Jesus (Jn 17:7).
- Identification of the specific group Jesus was praying for: The disciples whom the Father had given Him (Jn 17:9). Jesus clarified that He was not praying for the people of the world (Jn 17:9).
- Reasons Jesus singled out the eleven for prayer: Glory came to Jesus through them (Jn 17:10); Jesus was leaving the world for the Father and they would remain in the world (Jn 17:10).
- 1st Petition: "Father, protect them by the power of your name" (Jn 17:11). Jesus petitioned the Father to exercise protective oversight over His disciples in order to protect them from evil.
- Reason for the petition: "...so that they may be one as we are one" (Jn 17:11).
- Additional information: While Jesus was in the world, He had protected His disciples by the power given to Him by the Father. Except for Judas, not one of them was lost. Jesus was going to return to the Father so now the disciples needed the Father's protection (Jn 17:12-13). The disciples had been given God's words to share to a needy world; however, the world's system hated the disciples (Jn 17:14).
- 1st Petition clarified: Jesus had asked the Father to protect the disciples (Jn 17:11). Jesus clarified His petition. He was not asking the Father to remove them from the world, put to protect them while in it (Jn 17:15).
- Reason stated for 2nd petition: The disciples didn't belong to the world (Jn 17:16).

- 2nd Petition: Sanctify the eleven disciples (Jn 17:17). Jesus petitioned that the eleven disciples be set apart for their God-ordained mission in the world.
- Explanation of how the petition should be accomplished: Sanctify them through the Father's truth (Jn 17:17).
- Explanation of Jesus' effort to accomplish the petition: Jesus had sanctified himself in order to make the disciples' sanctification possible (Jn 17:19).

3rd **Jesus prayed for future believers.** Jesus broadened in scope His prayer to include all who would believe through the eleven disciples' words. Jesus did not make new petitions for them; however, He included them in the two petitions He had made for the eleven (Jn 17:20).
- Purpose of Jesus' petitions: That they may all be one (Jn 17:21). Jesus did not petition the Father to make all people believers, but He petitioned that all believers be kept in God's name (Jn 17:11), and sanctified in God's truth (Jn 17:17) so that they all may be one (Jn 17:21). If the Father grants the two petitions, unity will be a reality.
- Reason unity among believers was necessary: So that the world may believe that the Father had sent Jesus and that the Father loves believers in the same way that He loved Jesus (Jn 17:23).
- <u>Observation</u>: *Jesus did not pray for the salvation of unbelievers. However, He prayed directly for His eleven disciples and future believers so that unbelievers might be saved.*

4th **Jesus concluded His prayer**
- Expression of a two-fold desire:
  1st desire: That believers should be with Him (Jn 17:24).
  2nd desire: That believers should behold His glory (Jn 17:24).
- Father addressed as "Righteous Father" (Jn 17:25).
- Final observations: The world does not know God the Father, but Jesus does and His disciples and believers understand that fact (Jn 17:25). Jesus had in the past and would in the future reveal the Father to the disciples and believers so that they would experience the love the Father had for Jesus and that Jesus would be in them (Jn 17:25-26).

Applications:
- Jesus addressed God as "Father," and so should we. Jesus knew God intimately and personally as Father, and so can we.
- If we imitate Jesus' prayer, we will make specific petitions, and we will back up our petitions with sound reasoning, explaining why we need those specific requests to be granted. We will discuss why we are making the petition, what the petition involves, and the ultimate purpose of the petition.
- Like Christ, we need to be specific with respect to those for whom we pray.

Jesus' Prayer in Gethsemane Matthew 26:36-46; Mark 14:32-42; Luke 22:39-46

About midnight, early Friday morning, Jesus and the disciples arrived at a garden called Gethsemane. Jesus told His disciples, "Sit here while I go over there and pray."

Jesus took Peter, James, and John with Him. Jesus felt an agonizing distress, and told the three, "My anguish is so great that it's almost killing me. Stay here and keep watch."

Jesus went a little farther and fell facedown to the ground and prayed, "Father, everything is possible for you. Take this cup of suffering from me. Yet let your will be done rather than mine" (Mat 26:36-39; Mk 14:32-36).

Jesus was in such anguish, and He prayed so earnestly that His sweat was like drops of blood falling to the ground (Lk 22:44).

Jesus returned to the three disciples and found them sleeping. Jesus told Peter, "Couldn't the three of you keep watch for one hour? Watch and pray so that you won't fall into temptation. The spirit is willing, but the body is weak."

Once more Jesus went away and prayed the same prayer, "Father, everything is possible for you. Take this cup of suffering from me. Yet let your will be done rather than mine." Jesus returned to the three and once again found them sleeping. Jesus went away again and prayed the same words as before.

Returning the third time, Jesus told the three disciples, "Get up. Let's go! Here comes my betrayer!" (Mat 26:40-46; Mk 14:37-42).

Commentary:
Jesus left His disciples and went to a secluded place in the garden for the purpose of praying.

Jesus experienced emotional distress and He told His disciples about it – He was overwhelmed with sorrow (Mat 26:38); He became deeply distressed and troubled (Mk 14:33-34). Jesus' prayer battle was so intense that it was physically manifested in the form of a bloody sweat. Facing emotional distress, Jesus deliberately withdrew from His disciples and sought solitude in order to pray.

Jesus fell with His face to the ground. Jesus falling on the ground face-down indicates a desperate struggle.

Jesus' prayer:
- Addressed to: "My Father."
- Petition: "...if it is possible, may this cup be taken from me" (Mat 26:42 NIV). Jesus petitioned to escape from the "cup." In the Old Testament, "Cup" was figurative for God's wrath (for example see Psalm 75:8). Jesus desired to escape the cross. Jesus did not question God's ability to free Him from the cross; He questioned if God would be willing to do so.
- Declaration: "Yet not as I will, but as you will " (Mat 26:39 NIV). Jesus desired the Father's will above all else.
- Repetition: Jesus prayed the same prayer three times.
- Results: Christ entered the garden disturbed and distressed. He left the garden in command of the situation and remained in control and calm throughout His arrest, trial, and crucifixion. When Jesus began His prayer, He was emotionally distressed. After His prayer, Jesus left the garden confident to face the cross.

Applications:
- The person who is experiencing a crisis should be honest and express his true feelings. In the garden, Jesus expressed His emotional suffering to His disciples (Mat 26:38; Mk 14:33-34).
- Crisis situations should prompt solitary prayer with precise and definite petitions.

- When God's answer to prayer is different from what a person requests, one should accept God's will. Jesus asked to be freed of the "cup" of the cross (Lk 22:39-46). Afterwards, He submitted to God's will and faced the cross.
- It is legitimate to bring the same prayer request over and over to the Father. Repeated earnest petitions are different from vain repetitions.

Jesus' Three Prayers from the Cross

- **Jesus' Prayer for His Persecutors** Luke 23:34

"Jesus said, 'Father, forgive them, for they do not know what they are doing'" (Lk 23:34 NIV).

Commentary:
- Address of prayer: "Father."
- Petition: Forgive them.
- Reason for petition: They don't know what they are doing. The petition was for the Roman soldiers who were engaged in the Crucifixion. Jesus petitioned for them because they were ignorant of their actions. However, the Jewish leaders and the people of Jerusalem who shouted "Crucify Him," knew what they were doing.

Applications:
- When a need arises, prayer should be a spontaneous reaction.
- Christians facing crisis should be aware of the spiritual needs of others. When Jesus was suffering at Calvary, He was aware of the spiritual needs of the Roman soldiers.
- Petitions to God should be accompanied with an explanation of the reason for the petitions. Almost always, Jesus explained to His Father the reason for making a petition.

- **Jesus Prayed for Himself** Matthew 27:46; Mark 15:34

"About three in the afternoon Jesus cried out in a loud voice, 'Eli, Eli, lema sabachthani?'" (which means, "My God, my God, why have you forsaken me?" (Mat 27:46 NIV). Jesus' prayer was a quotation of the first verse of Psalm 22.

Back-story:
Jesus was nailed to the cross about 9:00 a.m. He was ridiculed by the people, the religious leaders, the soldiers, and by one of the robbers who was also on a cross. There was total darkness from noon until 3:00 p.m. Jesus uttered this prayer around 3:00 p.m. (Mat 27:45).

Commentary:
- Jesus shouted out His prayer (Mat 27:46). This indicates Jesus was in agony.
- Address of prayer: "My God!" Jesus directly addressed God. All other prayers of Jesus were addressed to "Father."
- Jesus questioned God, "My God, my God, why have you forsaken me?" (Mat 27:46). The idea of the prayer is: "For what purpose have you abandoned me?"
- When Jesus faced agony beyond His understanding, He cried out in prayer.
- Jesus prayed Scripture back to God. His prayer quoted the first verse of Psalm 22.

Applications:
- It is legitimate to question God in prayer. We should be honest with God and confess our confusions and questions to Him.
- Scripture that expresses our thoughts, needs, or emotions needs to be prayed back to God.
- Our reaction to turmoil and confusion should be to cry out to God in prayer.

- **Jesus' Prayer of Dedication** Luke 23:46
"Jesus called out with a loud voice, 'Father, into your hands I commit my spirit.' When he had said this, he breathed His last" (Lk 23:46 NIV). This is a quotation of Psalm 31:5.

Back-story

Jesus' prayer "My God, my God, why have you forsaken me?" (Mat 27:46) was misunderstood by witnesses to the crucifixion as a cry to Elijah. Then a man taunted Jesus by giving Him some vinegar to drink. Shortly afterwards, Jesus shouted His words of consecration; then He died (Lk 27:46).

Commentary:
- Jesus prayed Scripture back to God. His prayer quoted Psalm 31:5.
- The prayer was Jesus voluntarily giving His spirit to the Father. His was a prayer of dedication, consecration, and submission.
- In a time of crisis and confusion, Jesus trusted God enough to totally commit himself to God.
- Shortly after Jesus' heartbreaking cry, "My God, why have you forsaken me?" (Mat 27:46), Jesus shouted out this prayer of confident victory in a loud voice. This implies that the Father answered Jesus' desperate cry; even though, the Scripture does not state that God did.

Applications:
- Scripture that expresses our thoughts, needs, or emotions needs to be prayed back to God.
- In time of crisis, earnest prayers are emotional prayers.
- When we face a crisis and we experience confusion, we still need to trust God enough to dedicate ourselves to God, consecrate ourselves to honor God during the crisis, and submit ourselves to do His will.
- We need to trust God enough to pray a prayer of dedication. We need to confess that in every area of our lives we belong to God the Father, and we dedicate ourselves to go where He wants us to go, do what He wants us to do, and be what He wants us to be.

Thief's Prayer from the Cross Luke 23:39-43

One of the two criminals who hung on one of the crosses next to Jesus hurled insults at him, "Aren't you the Messiah? Save yourself and save us!"

However, the other criminal rebuked him, "Don't you fear God, since you're under the same punishment? We're getting what our deeds deserve. But this man has done nothing wrong."

Then the criminal said, "Jesus, remember me when you come into your kingdom."

Jesus answered the criminal, "I tell you the truth, today you will be with me in paradise"(Lk 23:39-43).

Commentary:
Jesus was being crucified. His disciples had fled or lingered disillusioned at the edge of the crowd. The chief priests, scribes, Jewish leaders, and the multitude were condemning and scorning Jesus. But the condemned man, who also was dying on a cross, looked across and saw not another dying man, but the Messiah himself. He understood that Jesus was not an impostor, but that He would receive the Kingdom that belongs to the Messiah. And the dying thief prayed a prayer of repentance. Some steps to the thief's repentance are:
- His concern about his companion's wickedness in scorning Christ. "Don't you fear God?" (Lk 23:40).
- He confessed his own sin, "We are punished justly, for we are getting what our deeds deserve" (Lk 23:41).
- He confessed Christ's innocence. "This man has done nothing wrong" (Lk 23:41).
- He confessed his faith that Jesus had a kingdom (Lk 23:42).
- He prayed, asking Jesus to remember him (Lk 23:42).

Applications:
While a person is alive, it is never too late to pray the prayer of repentance.

Peter and John's Prayer Acts 4:23-31
"'Sovereign Lord,' they said, 'you made the heavens and the earth and the sea, and everything in them. You spoke by the Holy Spirit through the mouth of your servant, our father David: 'Why do the nations rage and the peoples plot in vain? The kings of the earth rise up and the rulers band together against the Lord and against his anointed one.' Indeed Herod and Pontius Pilate met together with the Gentiles and the people of Israel in this city to

conspire against your holy servant Jesus, whom you anointed. They did what your power and will had decided beforehand should happen. Now, Lord, consider their threats and enable your servants to speak your word with great boldness. Stretch out your hand to heal and perform signs and wonders through the name of your holy servant Jesus.'"

"After they prayed, the place where they were meeting was shaken. And they were all filled with the Holy Spirit and spoke the word of God boldly" (Ac 4:23-31 NIV).

Back-story:
Peter and John went to the temple and healed a 40-year-old crippled who was begging for money. It was faith in the name of Jesus that gave the man complete healing. The people were astounded. Peter then accused the people of killing Jesus, but declared that God raised Him from the dead. Peter appealed for the people to repent and turn to God. The Jewish religious leaders put Peter and John in jail. The next day, the religious leaders questioned Peter and John. Peter, filled with the Holy Spirit, answered that it was by the name of Jesus, whom they had crucified, but whom God had raised from the dead, that this man stood healed. Salvation is found in no one else but Jesus. The religious leaders couldn't deny the miracle, but told Peter and John not to speak in the name of Jesus. After threats, the religious leaders let them go. Peter and John returned to the believers and reported all that the religious leaders had said to them.

Commentary:
After the Sanhedrin Council threatened Peter and John, the church met, praised God as the Sovereign Lord, and, in prayer, mentioned the events that had happened, and requested courage to continue speaking the Word of God (Ac 4:23-31).

Application:
When believers suffer persecutions or threats, the appropriate reaction is to praise God and, in prayer, ask God for courage.

When believers suffer a crisis situation, they should pray with a positive faith, and they should trust in the power and love of God, in spite of life's circumstances.

Stephen's Prayer of Forgiveness for Those Who Stoned Him
Acts 7:60

"While they were stoning him, Stephen prayed, 'Lord Jesus, receive my spirit.' Then he fell on his knees and cried out, 'Lord, do not hold this sin against them'" (Ac 7:60 NIV).

Back-story:
Stephen did miraculous signs among the people. Members of the Synagogue of the Freedmen were defeated by his arguments. They seized Stephen and brought him before the Sanhedrin. Stephen defended himself by telling stories about Abraham, Joseph's brothers selling him as a slave, the Israelites going to Egypt, their oppression in Egypt, Moses being brought up by Pharaoh's daughter, Moses living in the desert of Midian for forty years, God sending Moses back to Egypt to deliver the Israelites, their ancestors refusing to obey Moses, the tabernacle that was made as God directed Moses, the temple built by Solomon (Ac 7:1-50).

Stephen accused his listeners of being like their fathers who always resisted the Holy Spirit and persecuted the prophets. He accused them of betraying and murdering the Righteous One. His listeners dragged him out of the city and began to stone him (Ac 7:51-58).

Commentary:
Jesus taught His followers to pray for those who persecuted them (Mat 5:44). Jesus prayed for those who crucified Him (Lk 23:34) and Stephen, the first martyr, prayed to forgive those who were guilty of murdering him (Ac 7:60).

The person who is full of the Holy Spirit will imitate Jesus in his prayer life. Stephen was full of the Holy Spirit (Ac 7:55) and he died like Christ, praying to forgive those who were guilty of murdering him (Ac 7:60 with Lk 23:34).

Application:
We need to imitate both Jesus and Stephen by praying for those who wrong us.

The Church Prayed for Peter Acts 12:5-10

The early church in Jerusalem prayed for Peter after his arrest by King Herod, and God miraculously answered their prayer by sending an angel to free Peter from prison (Acts 12:5-10).

Back-story:

King Herod had the Apostle James killed. Then Herod put Peter in prison. The church prayed to God for Peter. The night before Peter was to go to trial, Peter was sleeping between two soldiers, bound with two chains. Guards were on duty at the door. Suddenly, an angel of the Lord appeared and woke Peter up. The angel said, "Quick, get up!" The chains fell off Peter's wrists.

The angel told Peter, "Put on your clothes and sandals, and follow me." The angel and Peter passed the guards and came to the iron gate leading to the city. The gate opened for them and they went through it. Suddenly, the angel left Peter. Peter went to the house where many people were gathered to pray, and he told his story about how the Lord rescued him out of prison (Ac 12:1-17).

Commentary:

God answered the church's prayers and orchestrated Peter's release from prison (Ac 12:7-10).

The church responded to a crisis situation by praying. When James was murdered and Peter arrested, the church met to pray (Ac 12:12).

God's ways are mysterious. The Bible does not explain why God allowed King Herod to kill James, and, yet, God miraculously saved Peter (Ac 12:1-11).

Application:

When Christians experience crisis because they serve God, the church should respond by praying.

We may never understand why God allows some believers to suffer, but rescues others from suffering.

Apostle Paul's Prayers

Romans 1:8–10

"First, I thank my God through Jesus Christ for all of you, because your faith is being reported all over the world. God, whom

I serve in my spirit in preaching the gospel of his Son, is my witness how constantly I remember you in my prayers at all times; and I pray that now at last by God's will the way may be opened for me to come to you" (Rom 1:8-10 NIV).

Commentary:
- Paul's prayer addressed to: "My God." Paul addressed God as his personal God.
- The mediator who gave Paul access to his personal God was Jesus Christ. Paul's prayer to God was through Jesus Christ (Rom 1:8). The words "through Jesus Christ"; in essence, summarizes the epistle to the Hebrews which teaches that Jesus Christ is the believer's Great High Priest, through whom the believer has access to the throne of God the Father (Heb 2:17, 18, 4:14-16, 10:19-22). Jesus Christ is the one and only Mediator between God and people (1 Tim 2:5).
- Prayer of thanksgiving was of primary importance to Paul: the first thing Paul emphasized to the Romans is that he thanked God through Jesus Christ for all of them (Rom 1:8). Paul gave thanks for what God had done for and through himself, but also gave thanks for what God did through other believers.
- Specific reason for his thanksgiving: their faith was proclaimed throughout the whole world (Rom 1:8).
- Clarification: God, whom Paul served in preaching the gospel of His Son, can witness that he continuously prayed for the Romans (Rom 1:9-10).
- Prayer request: Paul's prayer request was that he might finally succeed in visiting the Romans (Rom 1:10). Paul desired a successful journey to Rome. The book of Acts describes the answer to Paul's request: Paul went to Rome as a prisoner after he was arrested in the temple in Jerusalem and was falsely accused by Jewish authorities. Then Paul was a prisoner for several years. On Paul's trip to Rome, he experienced a terrible storm at sea, the ship was lost, and then wrecked. Paul made it to land, and was bitten by a snake. When he got to Rome, he was under house arrest.

- A condition that must exist for his prayer request to be answered: God's will (Rom 1:10). Paul's petition was that if it were God's will for him to visit the Romans, that the way be opened for him to go to them.

Application:
- Giving thanks to God should be a primary emphasis of our prayers. See Ephesians 5:20 and Colossians 3:16-17.
- We pray to a personal God. He is our God.
- Prayer bridges the gap that separates us from other people because of distance, culture, misunderstanding, or estrangement.
- Paul's prayer for the church at Rome reminds us that prayer is a primary work of the spiritual leader.
- In prayer we seek to align ourselves with God's will instead of trying to get God to align himself with our will.

Romans 10:1

"Brothers and sisters, my heart's desire and prayer to God for the Israelites is that they may be saved" (Rom 10:1 NIV).

Back-story:

Romans chapters 9 - 11 deal with a problem Jewish Christians grappled with that may seem foreign to us. Converted Jews in the first century questioned some things that happened under the power and influence of the gospel:
- Annulment of the Law of Moses.
- Inclusion of non-Jews in God's family.
- End of the Jewish theocratic system.

Romans chapters 9 - 11 deal with these problems and questions entertained by Paul's Jewish readers.

Paul stated the issue in Romans 11:1, "Did God reject his people?" Apparently some converted Jews thought that God had rejected and pushed aside the Jewish nation. In Romans 9, 10, and 11 Paul shows that God had not rejected every single person with Jewish blood. Paul emphasized that God doesn't confer salvation on nations, but on individuals who choose to obey Christ, whether they are Jews or non-Jews. Individual Jews who were lost, were lost because of their own unbelief and disobedience.

Paul begins Chapter 10 the same way as Chapter 9; Paul expresses his personal pain and concern for his Jewish countrymen. The fact that Paul's own people were lost was a heavy weight on his heart.

Paul recognized that the Jews had a zeal for God, but their zeal was not based on the knowledge of God (Rom 10:2). The apostle Paul, before his conversion, exemplified such misdirected zeal. He perceived Christ and Christians as enemies of the faith of his fathers. Paul was responsible for throwing many of them into prison, and some were even put to death as a result of his zeal. Paul could not tolerate anyone who thought differently from the way he did. God had to strike Paul down on the road to Damascus (Ac 9:1-20).

In Romans 9:3, Paul gives ample proof of his concern for their salvation because he was willing to become a sacrifice for their welfare. Paul was distressed because his fellow Jews stumbled at that stumbling stone of faith (Rom 9:32-33). Paul knew that the Jews were being rejected by God because of their own obstinacy. However, God still waited to be gracious toward them, if they would only repent and turn to Him.

Commentary:

Paul's heart's desire for Israel translated into concrete action: Paul prayed to God for Israel. Paul didn't just "care", he prayed. Paul expressed his heart's desire to God in prayer.

Paul had no desire that his kinsmen should be destroyed; he prayed for them that they might return to God.

Application:

Christians should be concerned for and pray for religious people who have a sincere zeal that is misdirected because they lack a true knowledge of God. Some religious people do not obey the teachings of Christ, but they manifest an obvious zeal for religion, and are hostile towards those who disagree with them.

Paul exemplifies the proper attitude of Bible teachers and preachers who proclaim the truth that people who do not believe in Jesus are lost. They should both desire and pray for the salvation of the lost.

Deep concern for others should result in the action of praying for them.

Romans 15:5–6

"May the God who gives endurance and encouragement give you the same attitude of mind toward each other that Christ Jesus had, so that with one mind and one voice you may glorify the God and Father of our Lord Jesus Christ" (Rom 15:5–6 NIV).

Back-story:

Paul addresses the potentially divisive issue of how the stronger and weaker believers in Rome should learn to get along and build up one another (Rom 14:1 - 15:13). The stronger believers were mostly non-Jews who understood that in Christ, Christians have been freed from observing the Mosaic Law. They did not have scruples regarding kosher meat or Sabbath laws. But the weaker believers were mostly Jewish Christians who could not shake off these things with a clear conscience. A potential split could have divided the church along racial lines of non-Jews against Jews.

For Paul, it was crucial that there not be a separation of non-Jewish and Jewish churches. It is to God's glory when non-Jew and Jew, circumcised and uncircumcised, barbarian, uncivilized person, slave and free person (Col. 3:11) could set aside their differences and all come together in Christ as their all in all.

Commentary:

Paul's prayer was addressed to God who gives:
- Endurance – the ability to continue doing right.
- Encouragement – the push to give people courage to make a change in action, feeling, or belief so they do the right thing.
- Spirit of unity – the harmony that is the result of not judging others about matters of opinion and conscience and to judge oneself first in the Lord.

Paul's prayer request:
- That God would give them the same attitude of mind toward each other that Christ Jesus had – that they would be like-minded with one another by becoming like-minded with Christ.

The results of Paul's prayer being answered:
- They, with one mind and one voice, would glorify the God and Father of their Lord Jesus Christ – they would

experience the spirit of unity which proceeds from all having the same aim to be like Christ. This would result in God-glorifying worship. True Christian harmony surpasses differences in race, culture, age, gender, and background. It surpasses differences over secondary doctrines or practices. True Christian harmony comes from God, is based on Christ Jesus, and results in glory to God.

Application:
We need to pray for Christian harmony that surpasses differences in race, culture, age, gender and background, and that comes from God, is based on Christ Jesus, and results in God-glorifying worship.

We will have the same attitude as Paul toward one another when we have the same aim as Paul, to be like Christ; but not till then.

We need both to pray for and, with our actions, seek Christian harmony.

Romans 15:13
"May the God of hope fill you with all joy and peace as you trust in him, so that you may overflow with hope by the power of the Holy Spirit" (Rom 15:13 NIV).

Commentary:
Paul stated that non-Jews will hope in Jesus (Rom 15:12). In the next verse, Paul injected a prayer of benediction.
- Paul addressed his prayer to the God of hope (Rom 15:13). God is both the one who generates hope in us, and He is the object of our hope. "Hope" in the Bible refers to something certain, fixed, and unmovable. It is not a wish about the future; such as, "I hope it doesn't rain on our picnic tomorrow." Biblical hope carries an expectation of reality because it rests on God's promises; even if we haven't experienced the fulfillment yet. Biblical hope is the result of trusting the living God, who can be trusted to keep His promises, because of His character and faithfulness.
- Paul's prayer request: that the God of hope would fill them with all joy and peace (Rom 15:13). Paul didn't pray that

they would have a little bit of joy and peace trickling into their lives now and then. Rather, Paul prayed that they would be filled with all joy and peace so that they would overflow with hope. Paul wanted them to experience a continuous flow of joy and peace, similar to the way an artesian well overflows with water 24/7, 365 days per year.
- Paul clarified the human action required for them to be filled with joy and peace: trust in Jesus (Rom 15:13). They must keep believing in God and His Word. The results of believing is that it produces this joy and peace.
- The power of the Holy Spirit is the divine means of this abundant hope, joy, and peace (Rom 15:13). Hope is produced in the believer's mind by the agency and power of the Spirit of God. God the Father is the God of hope, but He gives hope to believers through God, the Holy Spirit.

Application:
Ask God to fill you and your fellow Christians to overflow with His joy, peace, and hope.

When we know God and His ways through His Word, we will know that He is completely trustworthy, and we will experience Spirit-produced hope, peace and joy.

We Christians have the privileges of joy, peace, and hope. God is the source, trusting Jesus Christ is the means, and the Holy Spirit is the agent.

We need a realistic view of Spirit-produced peace. It does not mean that we shrug off concern for difficult problems. Paul was filled with peace, yet he mentions the daily pressure on him "of concern for all the churches" (2 Cor 11:28). Biblical peace comes from taking our anxieties to God in thankful prayer (Phil. 4:6-7).

Paul's prayer that God fill the Roman Christians with joy and peace implies that there are degrees of joy and peace for Christians. Some Christians have a measure of these graces, but they do not abound in them. If there are different degrees of joy and peace, it is important for us to look to God for the fullest reception of these blessings.

The more we are filled with joy and peace, the greater will be our hope.

As I wrote this, I was concerned with my wife's declining health and my granddaughter's stage four cancer; however, I could still experience God-given and Holy Spirit-produced hope, joy, and peace.

2 Corinthians 12:7–9
"Therefore, in order to keep me from becoming conceited, I was given a thorn in my flesh, a messenger of Satan, to torment me. Three times I pleaded with the Lord to take it away from me. But he said to me, 'My grace is sufficient for you, for my power is made perfect in weakness.' Therefore I will boast all the more gladly about my weaknesses, so that Christ's power may rest on me" (2 Cor 12:7–9 NIV).

Commentary:
Paul's thorn in the flesh was some chronic physical infirmity that caused recurring attacks of acute pain. Paul had an illness when he arrived in Galatia, and the Galatians were willing to tear out their eyes and give them to Paul if it had been possible (Gal 4:13-15). Paul's thorn in the flesh was probably related to chronic eye problems.

- Paul addressed his prayers to the Lord (2 Cor 12:8).
- The reason Paul prayed: His chronic illness that he called a thorn in the flesh. This thorn turned Paul's attention to God. He pleaded with the Lord. Through the thorn, God brought Paul to himself.
- Paul's prayer request: That God would heal him of his chronic physical infirmity (2 Cor 12:8).
- Paul was persistent with his prayer request. Three times he pleaded with the Lord (2 Cor 12:8).
- God's answer: God did not heal Paul as requested, but gave Paul sufficient grace to live with his chronic infirmity (2 Cor 12:9). Essentially, the Lord told Paul, the Lord was the grace and the Lord was all the grace Paul needed. The thorn was not removed, but instead, Paul received God's grace which enabled him to endure the appointed purpose of the thorn.
- God's purpose for not answering Paul's prayer as requested: To prevent Paul from becoming conceited (2

Cor 12:7), and to use Paul's weakness to manifest Christ's power (2 Cor 12:9-10).

Application:
If Paul was in danger of spiritual pride, who among us can escape this danger?

We may not always receive the prayer-answer we desire from God. Paul begged God to heal him. God did miraculous things for Paul, such as curing him of a poisonous snake bite (Ac 28:3). Yet in this passage (2 Cor 12:7-10), Paul was not healed. Despite his desperate plea to God, the thorn in his flesh remained.

I hear teachings about prayer implying that unanswered prayers are the results of sin, lack of faith, or not praying the right way. I pleaded with God to give my wife better health -- request denied, her health deteriorated. I pleaded with God to show His mercy and free my wife from pain -- request denied. One night she woke me up screaming with pain, and she screamed for over two hours. It is most comforting to me to read Paul's remarks about God not answering his prayers. Paul's remarks should comfort other praying Christians whose prayers are not answered as requested.

We must emulate Paul's example by persistently going to God when we face undesirable painful experiences.

Just as God used Paul's thorn in the flesh to bring Paul to Him in prayer, painful experiences should bring us to God.

We need to tell God our desires just as Paul told God his desire to be healed.

Prayer itself can be a comforting experience. Even if we do not receive the answer we request, communion with God refreshes our souls and uplifts our spirits. The sweetest times of prayer often come in the middle of profound undesirable painful experiences.

Thorns in our lives should drive us to pray; however, we shouldn't wait until we feel that we are drowning in a storm before we seek God. Instead, we need to prepare for the unexpected storm by seeking God and His Word.

It is not our grace or strength or resources that are sufficient in times of a painful experience, but God's grace. Paul could not bear his thorn on his own, but God's grace enabled him to bear it. There will always be an abundance of God's grace for us. A fish in the ocean isn't worried about having enough water, and we don't need to worry about having enough of God's grace to face undesirable experiences.

It was on a Friday morning that I began to study Paul's prayer in 2 Corinthians 12:7-9. That Friday afternoon I picked up a U-Haul truck to help me move my wife into assisted living. As I drove the truck, I thought about Paul's thorn and his plea for God to remove it, and God's answer that His grace was sufficient. I cried out, "God, we need your grace to get us through my wife's declining health and her approaching death!" I remembered that God told Paul His grace was sufficient. Then I realized that we needed God's grace, and God's grace was all that we need to get through our present crisis.

Philippians 1:9–11
"And this is my prayer: that your love may abound more and more in knowledge and depth of insight, so that you may be able to discern what is best and may be pure and blameless for the day of Christ, filled with the fruit of righteousness that comes through Jesus Christ—to the glory and praise of God" (Phil 1:9-11 NIV).

Back-story:
My study of the opening thanksgivings and prayers of Paul's Epistles revealed to me that Paul always thanked God for what was strong in the church to which he wrote, and he prayed for God to supply that in which the church was weak. Paul's thanksgiving for his Philippian friends took place in the context of his praying for them (Phil 1:3-4). Paul spelled out the content of his prayer which included specific requests regarding the "good work" begun in them which he prayed God would bring "to completion" on "the day of Christ" (Phil 1:6).

Commentary:
The content of Paul's prayer:
- Prayer request: For their love to abound yet more and more. Paul wanted them to have a kind of love that placed a high value on another person and actively sought that person's benefit.
- Clarification of his prayer request: That this love would abound in knowledge and depth of insight. Paul prayed

that love would be accompanied by full knowledge of God and moral insight into what God wanted them to do.
- The reason for his request: So that they might discern what was best. Paul wanted them to evaluate, determine, and prioritize the things that really mattered. His request was not for them to distinguish good from bad, but good from the best; to focus their time and energy on what really mattered.
- The future results of his prayer being answered: They would be pure and blameless until the day of Christ's return. In ancient times, the biggest industry was the pottery industry. The cheapest pottery was thick and solid and did not require much skill to make. The finest pottery was thin and fragile both before and after firing. Often, the fine pottery would crack in the oven. Cracked pottery should have been thrown away, but dishonest dealers filled the cracks with a hard wax that would be undetectable in the shops. If the pottery was held up to sunlight, the cracks would show up darker. Paul desired for the believers to not cover up their flaws, but to be sincere, living with integrity, and not being hypocritical. To be pure means to be sincere, unmixed, without hypocrisy. To be blameless means to walk steadily without staggering and blundering.
- The immediate results of Paul's prayer being answered: They would now be full of the fruit of righteousness that comes through Christ Jesus.
- The final result of Paul's prayer being answered: The glory and praise of God. The ultimate goal of righteousness expressed by their ever-increasing love and knowledge is that they might live to the glory and praise of God through the work He was doing in their lives.

Paul's passion for the spiritual development of his people is revealed in his prayer for them. The focus of Paul's prayer was for their spiritual development to manifest itself in their ethical behavior.

Application:
Spiritual leaders need to imitate Paul and give thanks for the spiritual strength of people entrusted to our biblical nurturing and

pray for their weaknesses. We need to pray to God about their weaknesses before we talk to them.

Like Paul, our main prayers for those entrusted to us should be about their spiritual maturity and ethical behavior.

Biblical Christianity means loving God and others; however, such love must be in line with God's truth as revealed in the Bible. Love that is not based on truth is emotionalism and truth devoid of love results in arrogance. We must avoid two extremes if we desire to grow to Christian maturity:

- We must avoid love devoid of doctrine. Our emphasis on love should not result in avoiding truth that hurts.
- We need to avoid the other extreme that emphasizes knowledge and correct doctrine, without practicing biblical love. We must not restrict love so narrowly that we are cruel and harsh toward those who disagree with us on some minor point of doctrine.

Paul prayed that the Philippians would grow in discerning what was best. One of life's greatest challenges is knowing what to leave out, what to ignore, and what to emphasize. We are tempted to concentrate on what is good instead of what is best.

Ephesians 3:14-19

"For this reason I kneel before the Father, from whom every family in heaven and on earth derives its name. I pray that out of his glorious riches he may strengthen you with power through his Spirit in your inner being, so that Christ may dwell in your hearts through faith. And I pray that you, being rooted and established in love, may have power, together with all the Lord's holy people, to grasp how wide and long and high and deep is the love of Christ, and to know this love that surpasses knowledge—that you may be filled to the measure of all the fullness of God" (Eph 3:14-19 NIV).

Commentary:

Paul began abruptly with the phrase: "For this reason." Because Paul had been entrusted with revelation by the Spirit (Eph 3:1-13), Paul prayed that his readers may be strengthened in spiritual power, love, and knowledge (Eph 3:14-19).

Paul kneeled in prayer (Eph 4:14). See Acts 20:36; Acts 21:5. Stephen kneeled when he was stoned (Ac 7:60). Peter kneeled when he raised Tabitha from the dead (Ac 9:40).

Essentially Paul prayed for his readers to have four things:
- Inner spiritual strength and power through the Holy Spirit (Eph 3:16).
- The indwelling of Christ in their hearts because of their faith (Eph 3:17).
- The ability to understand all the dimensions of spiritual realities (Eph 3:18).
- Knowledge of the love of Christ (Eph 3:19).

Paul's reason for his four prayer requests: So that they could be completely filled with God (Eph 3:19).

Application:

When praying, we should be aware we are in the presence of the Lord God Almighty and should show respect in His presence.

Our prayers in favor of the church should be primarily for spiritual blessings.

We should use our minds to think when we are praying, and be able to give the reason for our prayer requests.

1 Thessalonians 3:9–13

"How can we thank God enough for you in return for all the joy we have in the presence of our God because of you? Night and day we pray most earnestly that we may see you again and supply what is lacking in your faith. Now may our God and Father himself and our Lord Jesus clear the way for us to come to you. May the Lord make your love increase and overflow for each other and for everyone else, just as ours does for you. May he strengthen your hearts so that you will be blameless and holy in the presence of our God and Father when our Lord Jesus comes with all his holy ones" (1 Thess 3:9–13 NIV).

Back-story:

Paul, Silas, and Timothy planted the church in Thessalonica. However, they remained in Thessalonica for about three weeks. They only went to the synagogue for three consecutive Sabbaths (Ac 17:2) before their preaching stirred opposition that forced them to leave the city (Ac 17:5-10.).

Paul and his colleagues were anxious about the church in Thessalonica. Paul sent Timothy to Thessalonica to strengthen the church members and to report back to Paul regarding the situation there (1 Thess 3:1-2). Timothy returned to Paul and reported good news about their faith and love (1 Thess 3:6-8).

Commentary:
1 Thessalonians 3:9-13 is divided into two sections:
1st Paul's report on his prayer for the Thessalonians:
- Paul and his companions could never thank God enough for all the gift of joy the Thessalonians gave them (1 Thess 3:9).
- Paul prayed fervently night and day to have the opportunity to visit and see them again (1 Thess 3:10), and to supply what they still needed for their faith (1Thes 3:10). Paul wanted the opportunity to finish the job of discipling the new Christians.

2nd Paul's prayer requests:
- For God the Father and the Lord Jesus to work as one to make it possible for Paul and his colleagues to visit Thessalonica again (1 Thess 3:11).
- That the Lord would greatly increase their agape love for each other and for everyone else (1 Thess 3:12). Agape love focuses on the welfare of the other person. Paul prayed that they would love others just as Paul, Silas, and Timothy loved them (1 Thess 3:12). Paul held up his own love as a standard for them to imitate in their love for others.

The end results of Paul's prayers being answered:
- God would establish their hearts blameless in holiness before God, who was their Father, at the coming of the Lord Jesus with all His saints (1 Thess 3:13). Paul wanted the Thessalonians to be ready for Jesus' Second Coming. To become holy, a Christian must separate himself from the sinful world into a deep abiding relationship with God so that he becomes more God-like and less like the sinful world-at-large.

Application:
Like Paul, spiritual leaders should become models of Christ who deserve to be imitated. Then they should pray that those under their care should obtain the Christlike characteristics that they themselves are modeling.

Leaders' prayers should include both thanksgiving for those under their care and supplications for their improvement.

The person praying needs to have a goal, the desired end results, that he desires to achieve through his prayers.

The spiritual leader should pray more for people's spiritual concerns than physical.

1 Thessalonians 5:23–24
"May God himself, the God of peace, sanctify you through and through. May your whole spirit, soul and body be kept blameless at the coming of our Lord Jesus Christ. The one who calls you is faithful and he will do it" (1 Thess 5:23–24 NIV)

Commentary:
- Paul addressed his prayer to: The God of Peace. It is God who gives peace. Paul had challenged the Thessalonians to live in peace with each other (1 Thess 5:13). But in his prayer, he emphasized that peace comes from God and God alone. God does not bestow His best blessings on Christians who are given to strife and disorder, but on those who are united by bounds of love.
- Paul's prayer request for the Thessalonians:
  - Complete sanctification. He prayed for them to be made holy in every way. Paul prayed for them to be separated from impure, defiled, or moral corrupt things, and to be made pure and wholly consecrated to God. The idea behind the word sanctify is "to set apart." A dress is a dress; but a wedding dress is sanctified - set apart for a special purpose. God wants Christians to be set apart for Him.
  - Preservation. He prayed for them to be found blameless when Jesus Christ returns. He desired for them to be completely without blame – including spirit, soul, and body.
- Paul was confident that his prayer would be answered because the Lord Jesus Christ who called them is faithful. God had called the Thessalonians to the saving knowledge of His truth, and the faithfulness of God was security that God would help them persevere to the end.

Application:
We need to be conscious of how characteristics of God relate to the prayer requests we take to God.

Spiritual leaders, when praying for those under their care, need to pray for God to do a work in their lives that God and God alone can do. We need to pray that they will become all that God would have them to become.

We can have enormous confidence in God because He is faithful to keep His promises.

God is at work to transform us Christians into the people He wants us to become. He ordained that we be like the Lord Jesus inside and out. And He is working to make us more like Jesus. We shouldn't doubt His purposes, even when we can't always see Him at work.

Knowing who God is gives us confidence in prayer. God is the God of Grace, the God of Love, the God of Peace, and He is the Faithful God who does what He promises.

Even when we pray for Christians to be faithful to God, we need to realize that our fidelity to God depends upon God's faithfulness to us.

2 Thessalonians 2:16–17

"May our Lord Jesus Christ himself and God our Father, who loved us and by his grace gave us eternal encouragement and good hope, encourage your hearts and strengthen you in every good deed and word" (2 Thess 2:16–17 NIV).

Commentary:
- Paul addressed his prayer to: Our Lord Jesus Christ himself and God our Father. Paul gave additional information to clarify to whom he prayed: Who loved us and by His grace gave us eternal encouragement and good hope (2 Thess 2:16).
  - God's love is the spring and fountain of all God's grace we have or hope for.
  - God's grace is the spring and fountain for our everlasting consultation. The spiritual encouragement God gives is everlasting, because God loves with an everlasting love.

- Paul's prayer requests for the Thessalonians:
  - That God would encourage their hearts (2 Thess 2:17). God had given them encouragement and Paul prayed for them to receive more encouragement.
  - That God would establish them in every good word and work (2 Thess 2:17). He prayed that God would strengthen them to do and say everything that is good. He wanted them to become stronger in good works and good words.

<u>Application</u>:

Both Jesus Christ and God our Father hear our prayers. We may and should direct our prayers, not only to God the Father, through the mediation of our Lord Jesus Christ, but also to our Lord Jesus Christ himself. We should pray in Christ's name unto the Father, not only as Christ's Father but as our Father.

Spiritual leaders should pray that those under their care will grow spiritually in both what they do and what they say. We need to pray that believers' words and actions go hand in hand to bring glory to God.

We need to pray for Christians going through difficult times, that they will grow in hope and encouragement. Believers have good reason to be encouraged because our hope is grounded on the love of God, and the everlasting faithfulness of God.

TYPES OF PRAYER

Different types of prayers are found in the Bible, some given by name and others by example. There is also variation in how people categorize various prayers in the Bible. Because prayer is talking with God, it can occur at any time and place, involve a variety of forms, continue as a conversation with God throughout the day, and can also include times of public prayer among believers.

In practice, most Christians use different types of prayer during their prayer times, and we can apply any of these types of prayers to all the situations that face us.

Here are the main types of prayers in the Bible.

1. **Corporate or Public Prayer**

The book of Acts gives many examples of corporate prayer. The disciples and the early church were involved in public prayer. In the first couple of chapters of Acts, it appears that believers in Christ came together mainly to pray.

After Jesus' ascension, the disciples all joined together constantly in prayer (Ac 1:14). Later, after Pentecost, the early church devoted themselves to prayer (Ac 2:42). Their example encourages us to pray with others. Decision making in the early church was accompanied by prayer. For example: prayer accompanied the choosing of the first deacons (Ac 6:1-6) and the church sending out the first missionaries (Ac 13:1-3).

2. **Private Prayer**

In Matthew 6:5-6, Jesus told His disciples to pray privately. Nothing is wrong with public prayer, but it is wrong to pray in public in order to be recognized and admired by other people. Jesus said that hypocrites pray out loud – and loudly – so that they can be seen by others. Private prayer is a time of personal communication with the Lord.

3. **Prayer of Faith**

Jesus promised, "Therefore I tell you, whatever you ask for in prayer, believe that you have received it, and it will be yours" (Mk 11:24). Notice that Jesus did not say when you will actually see the result of your prayer. When you pray in faith, God immediately answers your prayer. But it may take time for the answer to manifest itself, and God may answer in an unexpected way.

Observation:

This verse has been abused by some to berate those who pray and their prayers are seemingly not answered. Some believed that all prayer is answered in heaven as soon as it is prayed; therefore, if the praying person does not see an answer, it is because he did not "pull the answer down" in faith. This also comes from the Prosperity Gospel preachers. We need to pray that God's will be done and that includes His timetable and circumstances. If the requested answer does not come as expected, then we need to ask for grace to endure the need until God's will is done. We can have peace knowing that God hears our prayer, and we can trust Him to do what is right and according to His will.

The apostle James proclaimed that prayer offered in faith will make the sick well (Ja 5:15).

The prayer of faith is offered in confidence knowing that the Lord will answer. We can know that God answers prayers that are in agreement with His will (1 Jn 5:14). When our prayers are in agreement with His will, then we can have confidence of the prayer of faith. *However, we don't always know God's will, so we must leave the matter up to God who has the power to change circumstances and also the grace to help us endure waiting or even not receiving our desired answer.*

"Now faith is confidence in what we hope for and assurance about what we do not see" (Heb 11:1 NIV). Faith is real; it is tangible. It is evidence of things you can't see.

The prayer of faith is based on our confidence in God's Word. When we are sure that what we are praying for is God's will, the prayer of faith can be employed. The prayer of faith is knowing God's will, praying it, and receiving it from Him. God answers prayers, and He will answer our specific prayer in line with His Word.

4. **Prayer of Agreement**
"Again, truly I tell you that if two of you on earth agree about anything they ask for, it will be done for them by my Father in heaven. For where two or three gather in my name, there am I with them." (Mat 18;19-20 NIV).

Jesus told His disciples to seek reconciliation with the fellow believer who sinned against them (Mat 18:15-17). In the context of seeking reconciliation, when two people agree and petition the Father, God will answer the request. Jesus is present where two or three come together in His name, seeking reconciliation (Mat 18:19). The opposite is implied. Where professed believers are together, but they are not working to resolve personal conflict, they can't expect Jesus to be part of the conflict.

Jesus taught that where there is sin, confront it directly, one-on-one, face-to-face. If this does not resolve the problem, include someone else in the conversation, and if all else fails take it to the church as a whole. From individual confrontation to communal attention, the movement of the passage is a progression that follows the development of the conflict from its origins in individual matters to its conclusion at the community level.

In His teachings on reconciliation, Jesus included facts about the prayer of agreement. Jesus promised the small group seeking to resolve the sin problem that whatever they bound on earth would be bound in heaven, and whatever they loosed on earth would be loosed in heaven (Mat 18:18). Bind and loose refer to the judicial authority of gathered Christians to resolve conflict situations on the basis of biblical teaching. When believers follow biblical teaching to resolve conflict and other sin problems, their decision on earth is honored in heaven. Jesus also promised that anything that is agreed upon by two on earth will be done for them by the Father in heaven (Mat 18:19).

Jesus promised that where two or three are gathered in His name, He is there with them (Mat 18:20). Jesus moved away from teaching about the prayer of agreement, to teach about the small group that is trying to resolve the sin problem. Jesus is present where two or three are gathered in His name, not just where two or three agree in Jesus' name, but where two or three are gathered.

This indicates that when a small group gathers because of their mutual relationship with Jesus, Jesus is present, even if the two can't agree about a sin matter and how to handle it, but they are trying to resolve the problem because they all have in common their relationship with Jesus.

Given the context, the two or three gathered for prayer (Mat 18:19-20) must be the two or three witnesses (Mat 18:16). In Deuteronomy 17:6-7 the two or three witnesses were to be the first to cast stones to punish the guilty. Jesus taught that the witnesses to a believer's sin problem are to be the first to pray.

5. **Prayer of Petition** (*Supplication*)

"Do not be anxious about anything, but in every situation, by prayer and petition, with thanksgiving, present your requests to God" (Phil 4:6 NIV).

The petition prayer is what most people think of when they speak of "prayer." Petition prayer is between you and God. It is you asking God for a particular outcome. Petition means to beg someone to change something or to do something. A passionate zeal and felt need fuels the prayer of petition. A search for the word "petition" in the Bible shows almost 60 instances of the word. In most cases it is talking about the person petitioning God for something on their own behalf. It usually means a plea for personal help. Seldomly does the Bible refer to petitioning as supplication on behalf of others.

Hannah, the mother of the prophet Samuel, was barren up to the point of his birth. Hannah offered a prayer of petition. "And she made a vow, saying, 'Lord Almighty, if you will only look on your servant's misery and remember me, and not forget your servant but give her a son, then I will give him to the Lord for all the days of his life, and no razor will ever be used on his head'" (1 Sam 1:11NIV). Hannah was under a cultural stigma due to her having no children. Hannah's personal petition represented both her desire to have a child and to see her stigma removed.

Application
It is not being arrogant or self-centered to pray for one's own needs. Take your genuine requests for help to God.

6. **Intercessory Prayer**
Intercessory prayer is a request offered to God on behalf of another person, group, or situation. It may be general requests for things such as the church or the government, or it may be specific prayer requests based on your knowledge of an individual's needs. Entreat is another biblical word that is used in the same way as intercede.

"And pray in the Spirit on all occasions with all kinds of prayers and requests. With this in mind, be alert and always keep on praying for all the Lord's people" (Eph 6:18 NIV).

- Examples of Intercessory Prayer
    - Abraham interceded on behalf of the cities of Sodom and Gomorrah (Gen18:22-33).
    - Elijah and the prophets of Baal met on Mount Carmel for a competition to determine which god was the true God. The Lord God manifested himself (1 Kin 18:17-40). Then, Elijah interceded for the people by asking God to end the drought in Israel and to send rain. The drought ended with a heavy rain (1 Kin 18:41-46).
    - The prophet Daniel offered a prayer of intercession. First he confessed the sins of the people of Israel and Judah. Then, Daniel affirmed that God was just in judging and punishing His people (Dan 9:4-15). Then, Daniel offered a prayer of intercession on behalf of Israel for God to turn His anger and fury away from Jerusalem (Dan 9:16), for God to forgive them and to look favorably on His holy place (Dan 9:17-19).
    - All of John 17 is an intercessory prayer of Jesus on behalf of His twelve disciples and all believers (Jn 17).
    - King Herod had James the brother of John executed. Then he had Peter arrested. Many people from the church gathered in the home of Mary, the mother of John Mark to pray for Peter. An angel freed Peter from prison (Ac 12:1-18).

- Christ who died, was brought back to life, and is at the right hand of God in heaven making intercession for us (Rom 8:34).
- Paul told Timothy that intercessory prayer, as well as other types of prayer, should be given on behalf of all people (1 Tim 2:1).
- Paul made intercession on behalf of the Ephesians that the Father would give them the Spirit of Wisdom and Revelation, so that they might know Christ better (Eph 1:15-18). Paul practiced intercessory prayer.

Applications:
Essentials of effective intercessory prayer:
- <u>Be committed</u>. Samuel told the Israelites that he would not sin against the Lord by failing to pray for them (1 Sam 12:23). A promise to pray for someone, is a sacred commitment, and you have an obligation to keep your promise.
- <u>Be discreet</u>. If someone asks you to pray for them, do not share the request unless they give you permission. Gossip may be disguised as a shared prayer request. Intercessory prayer in a group can be a form of gossip in disguise. For example: "Lord, comfort our sister Sally Sue as she suffers from her husband's betrayal." A little gossip shared as an intercessory prayer can be devastating instead of helpful.
- <u>Be sensitive</u>. If someone suffered a traumatic event, they're exhausted with retelling their story to every person who asks. Demonstrate concern for others without asking questions that satisfy our curiosity but requires them to relive their painful experience. All we need to do is use the information we have and pray for them. If they want to talk about their traumatic experience, listen to them, but don't ask questions to satisfy our curiosity.
- <u>Be organized</u>. My experience is, prayer requests that are not written down are soon forgotten. Whenever you promise to pray for someone, make a note of it.

7. **Prayer of Praise and Worship**
The prayer of worship is similar to the prayer of thanksgiving. Both focus on God. However, the prayer of thanksgiving focuses on what God has done; the prayer of worship focuses on who God is.

Praise and worship bring us into the presence of God. Praising God in both the good and bad times affirms our faith in Him.

- Examples of Prayers of Praise and Worship:
  - The psalmist David expressed praise to God declaring reasons why God's name is majestic in all the earth (Psa 8:1-9).
  - The psalmist called on people to: shout for joy to the Lord; worship the Lord; to enter His courtyards with a song of praise; to praise His name. And he expressed praise: The Lord is good; His love endures; His faithfulness continues (Psa 100:1-5).
  - Jesus' model prayer for the disciples teaches us to honor God's name as hallowed (Mat 6:9; Lk 11:2).
  - The shepherds who had seen the baby Jesus reacted by glorifying and praising God for all the things they had heard and seen (Lk 2:20).
  - Jesus gave sight to a blind man. The blind man who was healed followed Jesus praising God. The people who saw this, praised God (Lk 18:43). Both the blind man who was healed and the people who witnessed the event prayed prayers of worship.
  - The church at Antioch practiced worship, fasting, and prayer in the same context. The church was worshiping and fasting when the Holy Spirit communicated for Barnabas and Saul (Paul) to begin their mission work. Then the church fasted and prayed and sent the two off on their journey (Ac 13:2-3).
  - In Philippi, Paul expelled the demon from a fortune-telling, demon-possessed slave girl. The slave girl's owners dragged Paul and Silas before Roman officers. The Roman officers ordered Paul and Silas to be beaten and thrown into prison. At midnight, Paul and Silas were praying and singing hymns of praise to God. An earthquake opened the prison doors. The jailer, supposing the prisoners had escaped, started to commit suicide. Paul

shouted that the prisoners were still there. The jailer asked what he must do to be saved. They told him to believe in the Lord Jesus. The jailer washed their wounds. He and his family were baptized, and he fed Paul and Silas (Ac 16:16-34). After being beaten, imprisoned, and put into solitary confinement with their feet in stocks, Paul and Silas prayed and sang hymns of praise to God (Ac 16:25).

Application:
   In the prayer of worship, you do not ask God to do anything or to give you something. You do not ask for direction, neither do you dedicate your life to obey what God has called you to do. Rather, you just praise the Lord; you tell Him how much you love Him and why you love Him.

8. **Prayer of Thanksgiving**

- Invitations to give thanks to God:
  - Come before God with thanksgiving (Psa 95:2; 100:4).
  - Give thanks to God and make your requests known to Him (Phil 4:5-6).
  - Pray with thanksgiving (Col 4:20).
  - It is God's will for us to pray in all circumstances with thanksgiving (1 Thess 5:16-18).

- Examples of people giving thanks to God.
  - God enabled the Israelites to cross the Red Sea and saved them from the Egyptians. Then Miriam gave thanks to God while playing her tambourine and dancing with joy. She was joined by the other Israelite women (Ex 15:20–21).
  - Hannah gave a prayer of thanksgiving to God because He granted her petition for a son (1 Sam 2:1–10).
  - David sang a song of thanksgiving to the Lord after the Lord rescued him from his enemies (2 Sam 22:1–51).
  - During his prayer of dedication for the temple, King Solomon thanked God for all He had done to provide for Israel (1 Kn 8:14–21).
  - Before Elizabeth became pregnant, she was barren and beyond child-bearing age. Elizabeth became pregnant with

- John the Baptist, and she thanked God for taking away her reproach among the people of Israel (Lk 1:24–25).
- Mary gave thanks to the Lord for being chosen to bear the incarnate Son of God (Lk 1:46–55).
- Ten lepers asked Jesus to heal them. Jesus sent them to the priests, and they were all healed as they went. Only one of the ten healed lepers returned to thank Jesus. The thankful person was a Samaritan, and Jews despised the Samaritans as racially inferior (Luke 17:11–19).
- Jesus gave thanks to His Father: Before feeding the 4,000 (Mat 15:36); during the resurrection of Lazarus, Jesus thanked the Father for hearing His prayer (Jn 11:41); when inaugurating the Lord's Supper, Jesus took bread and gave thanks and gave the bread to His disciples (Mat 26:26); then Jesus took the cup, gave thanks and offered it to His disciples (Mat 26:27).
- Paul thanked God for the believers in Philippi because of their partnership with him in the gospel (Phil. 1:3–5).

Application:

It is God's will for us to pray with thanksgiving. Praying with thanksgiving should be a regular part of our prayer life and not reserved only for times when we feel that things are going well or for one special holiday each year. We should always have an attitude of thankfulness.

Gratitude is an attitude that comes out of the habit of giving thanks.

As my wife, Doris, and I dealt with Doris' declining health and moving her into assisted living, we were determined to find things for which to be thankful. We were thankful for a doctor who cared for us and who had tears in his eyes when he gave bad news. When Doris was in the hospital, we gave thanks for nurses who cared for her. We gave thanks for the staff at the assisted living place and the kindness they showed Doris. We gave thanks that when Doris moved into assisted living, our home and other property sold quickly. We gave thanks to God for the support our sons and other family members gave us.

9. **Prayer of Consecration**

The prayer of consecration is a prayer dedicating a person, an event, or a circumstance to God or for His purposes.

- Examples of consecration
  - God blessed the seventh day and sanctified it (Gen 2:3).
  - Before giving the Ten Commandments, God told Moses to consecrate the people (Ex 19:10) and the priest who came near to the Lord (Ex 19:22).
  - God told Moses to anoint, ordain and consecrate Aaron and his sons to serve as priests (Ex 28:41; 30:30).
  - Before conquering the city of Jericho, God told Joshua that all silver, gold, and articles of bronze and iron were holy to the Lord and should go into the treasury of the Lord (Jos 6:19).
  - Hannah prayed a prayer dedicating her son Samuel to the Lord (1 Sam 1:24-28).
  - Jesus prayed a prayer of consecration and dedication. He prayed about the will of God and dedicated His will to do the will of the Father (Mat 26:39; Lk 22:41-42).
  - A conflict developed in the Jerusalem church. Greek-speaking Jews complained that Greek-speaking widows were neglected when food was distributed. The twelve apostles told the church to choose seven men to put in charge of the problem. But the apostles would devote themselves to praying and ministering God's Word (Ac 6:1-4). The seven men were chosen, and the apostles prayed and placed their hand on them (Ac 6:6).
  - The Holy Spirit told the church in Antioch to set apart Barnabas and Saul for the work for which God called them (Ac 13:2).
  - Christians are urged to offer their bodies as a living sacrifice, holy and pleasing to God (Rom 12:1).
  - It is God's will for Christians to keep away from sexual sin as a mark of their concentration to Jesus Christ (1 Thess 4:3).

Application:
- The personal prayer of consecration involves praying for the will of God to be done in our own lives and submitting

ourselves to do God's will. Jesus prayed the same prayer three times in the Garden of Gethsemane, so the prayer can be prayed many times. It is a recognition that in every area of our life, we belong to God. We dedicate ourselves to go where God wants us to go, to do what He wants us to do, avoid what He wants us to avoid, and to be what He wants us to be.
- The prayer of consecration can be made to dedicate oneself, other people, an event, or a location to God.
- When you need to make a decision and you are unsure of God's will, or if you face two or more godly alternatives and you are not getting a clear sense of direction, pray a prayer of consecration. In the absence of direct instructions, tell God, "Lord, I'm going to do option "A" unless you show me it is not your will. If this is not your will, make it clear to me because I dedicate myself to do your will."
- The Christian life is a series of consecrations that repeatedly dedicate every affair of life and every decision to be made to God. Knowing God's will includes a commitment to do God's will.
- While studying the prayer of consecration, I prayed with my wife dedicating her failing health as well as my reactions to it to the Lord. We committed ourselves to do His will as we faced her approaching death together.

10. **Prayer of Imprecation**

The word "Imprecation" is not found in the Bible. But it is a type of prayer that King David prayed. To imprecate means to curse or speak evil toward someone. David used this type of prayer as a form of showing agreement with God's judgment and sovereignty over evil.
- Examples of prayers of imprecation: Psalms 7; 35; 58; and 59.

Application:

It is my conviction that the New Testament discourages the use of prayers of imprecation. Jesus taught His followers to love our enemies and pray for those who persecute us (Mat 5:44). The context (Mat 5:38-48) implies that we are to love them and pray for their good.

11. **Prayer of Meditation**
Biblical meditation is the art of reflection, of pondering and going over a matter in one's mind. It is connected to Bible study in all its forms. Biblical meditation can't be done in a hurry. It requires an unhurried reflection upon God's truth. As a cow regurgitates and chews its cud, meditation involves thinking and rethinking on Scripture. The goal of biblical meditation is to internalize and personalize the Scripture so that its truth affects how we feel, think, talk, and act.

Joshua 1:8
"Keep this Book of the Law always on your lips; meditate on it day and night, so that you may be careful to do everything written in it. Then you will be prosperous and successful" (Jos 1:8 NIV).

Commentary:
The Lord told Joshua to meditate day and night on the Book of the Law, so he would be careful to do everything written in it (Jos 1:8).

Joshua was to keep the Book of the Law always on his lips (Jos 1:8). This indicates that Joshua was to verbalize Scripture.

Joshua was promised prosperity and success if he meditated on Scripture and was careful in obeying it (Jos 1:8).

Application:
The effect of meditating on the word of God and speaking it is that we may be careful to do everything written in it (Jos 1:8).

The person who meditates on Scripture should voice his understanding of Scripture to others.

The person who meditates on Scripture and observes it will experience prosperity and success. This is not talking about financial prosperity, nor success in every competition, nor success in every endeavor. The person may not prosper and be successful by worldly standards, but he will be according to God's standard.

Psalm 1:2
"Blessed is the one...whose delight is in the law of the Lord, and who meditates on his law day and night" (Psa 1:1-2 NIV).

The psalmist begins with the description of the righteous person (Psa 1:1-3). One of the characteristics is that the righteous person meditates day and night on the Law of the Lord (Psa 1:2).

The word "blessed" has the idea of happiness or contentment or privilege (Psa 1:1).

Commentary:
The blessed person delights in the law of the Lord. Throughout the Psalms, the phrase law of the Lord describes God's entire word, not just the "Law" portion of the first five books of the Bible. The righteous person is delighted with all of the Bible (Psa 1:2).

Application:
The righteous person is a blessed person who finds his delight in Scripture. And he thinks about Scripture both day and night. He takes a text and carries it with him all day long.

Psalm 119:48
"I lift up my hands to your commands, which I love, that I may meditate on your decrees" (Psa 119:48 NIV).

Commentary:
Two possible interpretations exist for the phrase, "I lift up my hands to your commands."
- 1st The psalmist could have been saying that he lifted up his hands as an expression of delight or joy. He didn't just think about God's commandments with calm contemplation; he got excited about them and outwardly expressed his joy.
- 2nd The psalmist could have been saying that he lifted up his hands as an expression of prayer. God's commands put him into an attitude of prayer, and he was expressing an attitude of reverence and devotion.

The psalmist meditated on God's decrees. When he was alone, he thought about God's word with deep and calm contemplation. Thereby, he obtained a better understanding of them and was in a better disposition and capacity to keep them.

Application:
We should find joy in hearing, reading, and studying God's word. And we should respond to Scripture with prayer. We also should think about God's word with deep and calm contemplation.

Psalm 119:97-100
"Oh, how I love your law! I meditate on it all day long. Your commands are always with me and make me wiser than my enemies. I have more insight than all my teachers, for I meditate on your statutes. I have more understanding than the elders, for I obey your precepts" (Psa 119:97-100 NIV).

Commentary:
The psalmist loved God's word. This inspires him to meditate on God's word. God's word was in his thoughts all day long. He kept reflecting on Scripture, contemplating it, and thinking deeply about it. The more he thought about Scripture, the more he loved it (Psa 119:97). The more he thought about Scripture, the less it became a restraint or a burden, and the more it became a comfort and a delight. Still other verses that describe the psalmist's meditations are found in Psalm 119:15, 23, 48, 78. The psalmist was similar to a young man who loves a young lady and keeps thinking about her. And, the more he thinks about her, the more his love grows.

Loving Scripture and constantly reflecting upon it produced benefits for the psalmist:
- He became wiser than this enemies (Psa 119:97).
- He gained more insight than his teachers (Psa 119:99).
- He gained more understanding than people with years of experience (Psa 119:100).
- He obeyed Scripture's guiding principles. (Psa 119:100).

Application:
We too will discover that the more we love Scripture, the more it will be in our thoughts. The more we think about Scripture, the more we will love it and the more it will influence our lives.

Suggestions for biblical meditation:
- Read and reread a text aloud several times. With each reading emphasize different words in the text.

- Rewrite the text in your own words.
- Think of a way to illustrate the text. What picture or story illustrates it?
- Think of ways to apply the text to your life. As a result of meditating on the text, how should you think, talk, or act differently?
- Pray through the text.
- Memorize the text.
- Find and read parallel texts. Discover what other Scripture says about matters dealt with in the text.

12. **Flash Prayer**

Flash Prayer occurs when a person sends up a quick prayer to God when an unplanned situation requires an immediate reaction.

Nehemiah became sad when he received the news that the Jews who had left captivity in Babylonia and returned to Jerusalem were enduring serious trouble and were constantly being insulted (Neh 1:1-3; 2:1). The king asked Nehemiah why he was sad. Nehemiah said he couldn't help being sad when the place where his ancestors were buried was in ruins (Neh 2:2). Then the king asked Nehemiah what he wanted (Neh 2:4). Nehemiah quickly, suddenly, and silently prayed to God before answering the king (Neh 2:4). He silently in his mind requested God to direct his thoughts and words, and to incline the king's heart to his request.

Nehemiah needed to give the king a quick answer; he had no time to consider possible answers and prepare; he had no time to get alone with God, so he flashed a prayer to God.

Application:

Sometimes we are faced with an unplanned situation that requires an immediate answer or action. We do not have time to get alone with God to pray, and neither do we have time to consider possible answers or actions. But we can and should send up a quick silent Flash Prayer to God.

13. **Crisis Prayers**
    - "In my distress I called to the Lord; I cried to my God for help. From his temple he heard my voice; my cry came before him, into his ears" (Psa 18:6 NIV).

- "God is our refuge and strength, an ever-present help in trouble. Therefore we will not fear, though the earth give way and the mountains fall into the heart of the sea, though its waters roar and foam and the mountains quake with their surging. Selah. There is a river whose streams make glad the city of God, the holy place where the Most High dwells. God is within her, she will not fall; God will help her at break of day. Nations are in uproar, kingdoms fall; he lifts his voice, the earth melts. The Lord Almighty is with us; the God of Jacob is our fortress. Selah. Come and see the works of the Lord, the desolations he has brought on the earth. He makes wars cease to the ends of the earth; he breaks the bow and shatters the spear, he burns the shields with fire. 'Be still, and know that I am God; I will be exalted among the nations, I will be exalted in the earth.' The Lord Almighty is with us; the God of Jacob is our fortress. Selah" (Psa 46:1-11 NIV).
- "Have mercy on me, O God, have mercy on me, for in you my soul takes refuge. I will take refuge in the shadow of your wings until the disaster has passed. I cry out to God Most High, to God, who fulfills his purposes for me (Psalm 57:1-2 NIV).

Application:
- Trust God in the midst of disasters and worldwide shaking. This is the time for Christians to arise, shine, and to show others the peace of God through our lives by living out our faith.
- Pray that the people of God shine His light even in the darkest of times. During disaster, be careful to live a godly life.
- During disaster, pray for the salvation of souls and share your faith. During disasters and times of difficulties, people are open to the Gospel.

14. **Prayer of Confession of Sin**

The Bible says all people have sinned and fall short of God's standard (Rom 3:23). The Bible also says that if we claim to have no sin we are fooling ourselves, refusing to admit the truth, and calling God a liar. However, if we confess our sins to Him, He will forgive us and cleanse us from all our sins (1 Jn 1:8-10).

To confess sin is to agree with God that a specific behavior was wrong. It is to call our behavior by the name that God himself calls it in the Bible. When we confess our sins, we agree with God and call our wrongdoings "sin."

- Bible verses about confession of sin
  - King David committed adultery and had Bathsheba's husband killed to hide his wrong doing. Prophet Nathan confronted David about his sin. David confessed that he had sinned against the Lord. Nathan replied that the Lord had taken away his sin (2 Sam 12:13).
  - After confessing his sin, David wrote, "Blessed is the one whose transgressions are forgiven, whose sins are covered. Blessed is the one whose sin the Lord does not count against them and in whose spirit is no deceit. When I kept silent, my bones wasted away through my groaning all day long. For day and night your hand was heavy on me; my strength was sapped as in the heat of summer. Then I acknowledged my sin to you and did not cover up my iniquity. I said, 'I will confess my transgressions to the Lord.' And you forgave the guilt of my sin" (Psa 32:1-5 NIV).
  - "Whoever conceals their sins does not prosper, but the one who confesses and renounces them finds mercy" (Pro 28:13 NIV).
  - Daniel was a youth when he was taken to Babylon after Jerusalem was captured. Daniel was elderly when he prayed to God and confessed the sins of the people of Judah. His prayer is found in Daniel 9:4-19. Daniel's confession included, "We have sinned and done wrong. We have been wicked and have rebelled; we have turned away from your commands and laws" (Dan 9:5 NIV). Daniel confessed the sins of his nation to God.
  - When John the Baptist was preaching, people went to him, confessed their sins and were baptized (Mat 3:6).
  - "Therefore confess your sins to each other and pray for each other so that you may be healed. The prayer of a righteous person is powerful and effective" (Ja 5:16 NIV).

- "If we confess our sins, he is faithful and just and will forgive us our sins and purify us from all unrighteousness" (1 Jn 1:9 NIV).

- Reasons to confess sins:
  - To have one's prayer heard by God. The psalmist said, "If I had cherished sin in my heart, the Lord would not have listened; but God has surely listened and has heard my prayer" (Psa 66:18-19 NIV).
  - To be forgiven. The Apostle John promised, "If we confess our sins, he is faithful and just and will forgive us our sins and purify us from all unrighteousness" (1 Jn 1:9 NIV).
  - To have power in prayer. The Apostle James said, "Therefore confess your sins to each other and pray for each other so that you may be healed. The prayer of a righteous person is powerful and effective." (Jam 5:16 NIV). *(James implied that the confession of sin and the prayer of faith together bring healing. James declared that a righteous person's prayer is powerful and effective. A person only becomes righteous when he confesses his sins to God.)*

Application:

We need to be specific in our prayer of confessing sin, not generic. Specifically tell God what we did wrong, agreeing with God by saying the same thing as God does about our wrong-doing. We need to own up to God that our thought or action was wrong.

We need to trust God and recognize that when we confess that we have sinned, we can know that God has forgiven us.

Just as God forgives us, we should forgive others (Mat 6:12).

One motive to resist temptation is the understanding that yielding to temptation would hinder our relationship with God, and to restore that relationship we would need to confess our sin.

15. **Targeted Prayer**

   Targeted prayer intensely focuses on one issue or subject.

- Examples of targeted prayer:
  - Nehemiah. The first chapter of Nehemiah records a historical event that happened about 450 years before

Christ. Nehemiah was a slave serving the Persian king as his cupbearer. Nehemiah heard from his brothers about the terrible condition of his homeland, Jerusalem. Nehemiah took action by targeting his prayer for the Israelites. He prayed to God day and night about the Israelites (Neh 1:6). His prayer is recorded in Nehemiah 1:4-11.
- Jesus. The night before Jesus' death, He prayed for His disciples (Jn 17:9) and those who would believe in Him through His disciples' message (Jn 17:21). Jesus prayed a targeted prayer for His followers in John 17:1-26.
- Paul dealt with a recurring health problem that he called a thorn in the flesh. On three different occasions, Paul prayed a targeted prayer begging the Lord to take it away from him (2 Cor 12:8).

Application:
A crisis often causes us to focus our attention and prayers on one issue. The first response to a crisis should be to take action by praying about the issue. The day before I focused on targeted prayer, I read a newspaper article about two couples who were going on a trip together, leaving at 4:30 a.m. It was dark when they started putting suitcases in the car. Suddenly, two youths appeared pointing guns at them and demanded their car-keys, their billfolds, and purses. One traveler cried out, "Save us, Lord Jesus, save us!" The other travelers joined in praying the same prayer. The robbers reacted by running away. Those travelers reacted to a crisis with a targeted prayer for God's protection.

Targeted prayer should be our reaction to decision making times, or a time of intense concern about a situation. At this time in my life, my wife has moved into assisted living and we've put our house up for sale. When it sells, I'll join my wife in assisted living. I've done a lot of targeted praying for the selling of our house.

16. **Prayer for Salvation of Non-believers**
- Prayers related to the salvation of non-believers
  - Jesus told His disciples that the harvest is plentiful but the workers are few. Jesus commanded His disciples to pray to the Lord of the Harvest to send workers to harvest His crops (Mat 9:37-38).

- The night before Jesus' death, He prayed for His disciples (Jn 17:9) and those who would believe in Him through His disciples' message (Jn 17:21). In Jesus' prayer found in John 17:1-26, Jesus prayed that those who believe in Him would have unity so that the world would believe that the Father had sent Him (Jn 17:21).
- Paul prayed for the Israelites to be saved (Rom 10:1).
- Paul was in prison and he asked the church at Ephesus to, "Pray also for me, that whenever I speak, words may be given me so that I will fearlessly make known the mystery of the gospel, for which I am an ambassador in chains. Pray that I may declare it fearlessly, as I should" (Eph 6:19-20 NIV).
- When Paul was in prison, he also asked the church at Colossae to, "Pray for us, too, that God may open a door for our message, so that we may proclaim the mystery of Christ, for which I am in chains" (Col 4:3 NIV).
- Paul advised Timothy to pray for all who have positions of authority and Paul stated that God wants all people to be saved and to learn the truth (1 Tim 2:1-4).

Commentary:

Paul prayed a generic prayer for the Israelites to be saved (Rom 10:1). Neither Jesus nor Paul prayed for specific non-believers to be saved. However, both prayed that believers' actions and attitudes would result in non-believers becoming believers. Jesus came to seek and to save the lost (Mat 18:12; Lk 19:10). But Jesus did not pray for non-believing people to believe and be saved. He only prayed for His disciples. He prayed for His disciples to have unity so non-believers would believe that the Father had sent Him. When believers are unified, non-believers will reach the conclusion that it is true what believers say about Jesus, and many will respond by becoming believers. The converse is also true: When believers lack unity and experience conflict, non-believers reach the conclusion that it is a lie what believers proclaim about Jesus. Jesus did not tell His disciples to pray for the salvation of non-believers; however, He told them to pray for the Father to send workers to harvest non-believers.

Paul was in prison with criminals when he wrote to the churches in Ephesus and Colossae. But Paul did not ask the churches to pray for the salvation of those sinful criminals. Paul asked the churches to pray that God would open the door for God's message, that Paul would have the right words to say, and he would have the courage to say them.

Application:
God desires that non-believers become believers and be saved from their sins. If we imitate Jesus and Paul, when we are concerned about the salvation of individuals who are friends and family, we will not name them in our prayers and plea for their salvation. Instead, we will pray for ourselves and other believers with whom they are acquainted. We will pray for the non-believers in the following manner:
- That the non-believers have relationship with believers who show their love for one another with unity. This will convince them that God the Father sent Jesus and that it is true what we believers say about Jesus.
- That God would open the door for us and other believers to communicate God's message to the non-believers.
- That when God opens the door for us to tell the non-believers about Jesus, we would have the right words to say.
- That when God opens the door for us to tell non-believers about Jesus and gives us the right words, we would have the courage to say them.

17. **Habitual Prayers**
It is good to have the habit of praying to God on a continual basis. "Pray continually... for this is God's will for you in Christ Jesus" (1 Thess 5:17-18 NIV).

"In the same way, the Spirit helps us in our weakness. We do not know what we ought to pray for, but the Spirit himself intercedes for us through wordless groans" (Rom 8:26 NIV). There will be times you don't "feel" like praying, as well as times when you will find yourself struggling with what to say.

Prayer can be hard work. If you wait until you "feel" like praying, you probably will seldom pray! Most people have been so influenced by non-Christian values, that they aren't interested in "discipline." They'd rather have instant results, techniques, "How-to" books, or anything but struggle, discipline, and hard work. You need to deliberately set aside time to pray, putting aside other things you would like to do. You need to discipline your mind, so you won't spend the whole prayer time looking out the window and thinking about other things.

But after all is said and done, you will have no regrets. In the end, you will be more like your "Father in heaven," and you will grow to love His will more and more.

I have found the following prayer guides to be helpful for my private prayers, for leading public prayers, and teaching others to pray. The prayer guides are helpful for the normal habitual everyday prayer. They combine several types of prayer into one prayer event.

PRAYER GUIDE FOR THE NORMAL HABITUAL PRAYER			
LOVE	THANKS	SORRY	PLEASE
Praise	Thanksgiving	Confession	Request
Adoration	Express gratitude	Admit wrongdoing	• Intercede • Petition
Praise God	Give thanks	Confess sins	• Intercede for others • Make personal petitions

- **Praise**

To praise is to adore God or worship Him for who He is. When we praise God, we tell Him why we love Him. We talk about God's attributes, not what He has done for us. A good way to start praising God is to complete the sentence, "I love you God for..." You can also give praises to each individual in the Trinity – "I love you Father for ..."; "I love you Jesus for ..."; "I love you Holy Spirit for ..."

- **Give Thanks**

To give thanks is to say "Thank you" to God for all that He has been recently doing, for what He is doing, and for what He will do.

A good way to start thanking God is to complete the sentence, "Thank you God for..."

- **Confess Sins**

  To confess our sins is to agree with God that a specific behavior was wrong. It is to call our behavior by the name that God himself calls it in the Bible. When we confess our sins, we agree with God and call our wrongdoings "sin." We need to specifically tell God what we did wrong, agreeing with God by saying the same thing that God does about our wrong-doing. We need to own up to God that our thoughts, words, or actions were wrong.

- **Request – Intercede**

  To intercede is to pray in favor of other people. It is to make specific requests for specific people. Included in our habitual prayer, we need to make specific prayer requests for other people. God commands that we pray for others, and our concern for others should motivate us to pray for them.

- **Request – Personal Petitions**

  To petition is to take your personal requests to God. We need to take our personal needs, concerns, and desires to God in prayer.

- **Listen**

  To listen involves both hearing God's spoken word and having a time of silence when praying for the purpose of giving attention to what God wants to communicate to us. During the time of silence, the person does not speak; however, he listens. The silent person, who is conscious that he is in God's presence, is open to receive communication from the Lord.
  - After freeing the Israelites from slavery in Egypt, God promised them, "If you listen carefully to the voice of the Lord your God and do what is right in his eyes, if you pay attention to his commands and keep all his decrees, I will not bring on you any of the diseases I brought on the Egyptians, for I am the Lord who heals you" (Ex 15:26 NIV).
  - When the voice of God was calling the name of the boy Samuel, the boy told God to speak because he was listening (1 Sam 3:10).

- The psalmist David advised to be still before the Lord and to wait patiently for Him (Psa 37:7).
- The psalmist encouraged the godly to be still and know that the Lord is God (Psa 46:10).
- On several occasions, Jesus told people to listen to Him (Mat 13:18; 15:10; 21:33; Mk 4:3; 7:14; Lk 9:44).
- Jesus praised Martha's sister, Mary, for listening to Him (Lk 10:39-40).
- A voice from heaven told the disciples to listen to Jesus (Mat 17:5).
- Jesus claimed that He is the Good Shepherd and His sheep will listen to His voice (Jn 10:2-5, 27).

Application:
 We live in a world with constant noise. The radio, TV, ringing phones, pinging i-pads, and/or crying children will interfere with our hearing God. We need to structure a time of silence when we are conscious of God's presence and desiring to hear what God has to communicate to us.

It is good to have a structure to follow for normal habitual prayer time. Different people will follow different structures. I'm going to include another example of a structure for a habitual prayer time. My son, Sam Day, wrote an article which describes the seven ways he looks to God in prayer. With his permission, I'm including this article he wrote.

OVERCOMING S.A.D.D. WITH 7 WAYS TO LOOK AT GOD IN PRAYER

I self-diagnosed myself as having *Spiritual Attention Deficit Disorder* (S.A.D.D.). I start out praying—"*Lord, thank you for this day…look—SQUIRREL!*" When my mother was home-schooling me as a missionary kid in Brazil, she always had to set my desk away from the window. I was constantly getting distracted. My challenge when praying to God is keeping my eyes on Him, instead of whatever squirrel my mind starts chasing.

I recently read a description of prayer John Stott wrote in his book, Christian Basics: An Invitation to Discipleship (pg. 92-96). It has given me a new focus in my prayer life, drawing me closer to God. I've adapted, changed, and expanded what he teaches into 7 types of prayers. Each type of prayer is LOOKING in a different direction—which is great for someone like me who gets bored just looking in one direction! Now that God is taking me deeper with Him through this new journey of prayer, I wanted to share this with you. I invite you to pray daily, looking to God in these 7 ways:

1. Look **UP** at God	Worship	Revel in the glory of God. "Ascribe to the Lord glory and strength" (Psa 29:1b NIV). Marvel at the wonder of who He is, and who He has revealed Himself to be. In your daily reading of the Bible, ask yourself—"What does this teach me about my amazing God?" Another idea is to sing or meditate on the lyrics of great hymns and worshipful songs that fix our attention on God's character and mighty works. As I write, I'm moved by "How Great Thou Art"…
2. Look **IN** at ourselves	Confession	Review your day, and ask the Holy Spirit—"Search me, God, and know my heart; test me and know my anxious thoughts. See if there is any offensive way in me…" (Psa 139:23-24 NIV). Confess any sin He brings to mind, and receive the purifying cleansing of His complete forgiveness (1 Jn 1:9). As a result, your heart becomes "whiter than snow" (Psa 51 NIV).

3. Look **DOWN** at what we need to let go	Forgiving yourself & others	Undoubtedly, someone will hurt, betray, or say something cruel about you. Let go of resentment, and choose to forgive those who have wronged you. Unless you forgive, you can't experience God's forgiveness (Mat 6:14-15). Instead of holding on to anger, pray for them, and ask God to bless them (Mat 5:44, Rom 12:14). Who do you need to forgive now? Sometimes the one you need to forgive is yourself. This means finally letting go of the shame, guilt and self-condemnation you've been holding on to for far too long. Remember His truth—"Therefore, there is now no condemnation for those who are in Christ Jesus" (Rom 8:1 NIV). In letting go we find freedom! (Gal 5:1)
4. Look **BACK** at our blessings	Thanksgiving	Worship and thanksgiving are different. In ***worship***, we praise God for <u>who He is</u>; in ***thanksgiving***, we express our gratitude for <u>what He has done</u> for us and others. The reason the Israelites kept falling into despair and sin in the Old Testament is that their forgetfulness led to ingratitude—"But they soon forgot what he had done and did not wait for his plan to unfold" (Psa 106:13 NIV). We teach our kids to say "thank you" when someone does something nice for them. Look back over your day, and tell God "thank you" for the blessings you experienced from Him. Being thankful is transformational, for as the martyr, Dietrich Bonhoeffer, asserted before dying under Hitler, "Gratitude changes the pangs of memory into a tranquil joy."
5. Look **OUT** toward those far from God	Evangelism	Who are those outside of an intimate relationship with God that you know? They may be unsaved, backslidden, or unchurched. May our hearts ache for the lost, as did Paul's—"Brothers, my heart's desire and prayer to God for them is that they may be saved" (Rom 10:1, ESV). As you pray for them, is God leading you to somehow be an answer to that prayer?

6.	Look **AROUND** at the needs you & others have	Petition & Supplication	Bring to the throne of God the needs you, your family and friends have. Unload your burdens at the nail scarred feet of Jesus—who demonstrated the full extent of his care and power for you at the cross. A word of clarification, as John Stott wisely said, "The purpose of petitionary prayer, then, is neither to inform God as though He were ignorant, nor to persuade Him as though He were reluctant. It is not to bend God's will to ours, but rather to align our will to his." Our petition resonates with Jesus', "Not my will, but yours be done" (Luke 22:42 NIV).
7.	Look **FORWARD** to your goals	Dreaming bigger	We all need to have some "growth goals." We have *becoming* goals and *achieving* goals. At times we are focusing on our personal development that enables us to become all God created us to be—such as stopping old habits and starting new ones, or learning a new skill, etc. Other times, we are focusing on accomplishing something that makes a significant difference in people's lives—such as through a ministry at church, or a high-value project at work, etc. Whatever your goal, pray God will empower you to accomplish it in such a way that brings great glory to Him! "Everyone was amazed and gave praise to God. They were filled with awe and said, 'We have seen remarkable things today.'" (Lk 5:26 NIV).

Looking to God in these 7 directions during prayer, has changed me from being S.A.D.D. to GLAD!

Application to habitual prayer:

It is good to have a structure to follow for normal habitual prayer time. You may structure your prayer time differently than my son or me, but I suggest you develop a plan to follow for your normal every day prayer time.

PRAYING THE SCRIPTURE

Praying the Scripture means reading, listening to, or remembering Scripture and then talking to God about the Scripture.

One way to know that our prayers are the will of God is to pray specific Scriptures that express what is in our hearts. Scripture should not be used as a magic chant (repeated mindlessly as though the words themselves had power). When we find a command or promise that expresses what is in our hearts, we know we are agreeing with God when we use it as a prayer. The more we listen to or read the Bible, the more it becomes part of us. Then Scripture comes to mind when we are praying and gives us the words we need when praying. When we don't know what to pray, Scripture can give us the words and put our thoughts into words.

Reasons for Praying the Scriptures
Praying Scripture back to God helps us to focus our minds and will assure that the subject matter of our prayers is pleasing to God. Praying the Scriptures prevents our prayers from degenerating into vain repetitions that eventually revolve entirely around our immediate private concerns, rather than God's larger purposes.

Jesus said, "If you remain in me and my words remain in you, ask whatever you wish, and it will be done for you." (Jn 15:7 NIV). This implies that a connection exist between our minds being shaped by Scripture and our prayers being answered.

God answers prayer petitions that His Son has a hand in initiating. "This is the confidence we have in approaching God: that if we ask anything according to his will, he hears us. And if we know that he hears us—whatever we ask—we know that we have what we asked of him" (1 Jn 5:14-15 NIV). Prayers that appeal to Scripture are aligned with God's will.

Biblical Examples of Praying the Scripture

Ezra, Nehemiah 9:6–37
Ezra's prayer in Nehemiah chapter nine is the longest prayer recorded in all the Bible. Ezra's prayer did not quote Scripture, but it summarized biblical history and many biblical texts:
- God as creator (Neh 9:6 // Gen 1-11)

- God's choice of Abraham (Neh 9:7-8 // Gen 12-50)
- God's actions in the Exodus (Neh 9:9-14 // Book of Exodus)
- God's faithful care and provision during the wilderness wandering period (Neh 9:15-21 // Book of Numbers)
- God's promises to Abraham fulfilled (Neh 9:22-25 // Book of Joshua)
- Israel's further rebellion (Neh 9:20-31 // time of the Judges)
- God's covenant faithfulness and Israel's unfaithfulness continue (Neh 9:32-38 // the time of the kings in Judah and Israel)

Application:
A prayer that summarizes biblical teaching or that is based on biblical principles is praying the Scripture. Praying the Scripture is not restricted to reading a Scripture text and talking to God about it, or reading a Scripture text to God in the form of a prayer.

Jesus prayed the Scripture twice when He was on the cross

- **Jesus prayed for himself** Matthew 27:46 & Mark 15:34 // Psalm 22

"About three in the afternoon Jesus cried out in a loud voice, 'Eli, Eli, lema sabachthani?" (which means 'My God, my God, why have you forsaken me?'" (Mat 27:46 // Psa 22 NIV). Jesus' prayer was a quotation of the first verse of Psalm 22. Jesus prayed Scripture back to God when He quoted the first verse of Psalm 22.

- **Jesus' prayer of committal** Luke 23:46 // Psalm 31:5

"Jesus called out with a loud voice, 'Father, into your hands I commit my spirit.' When he had said this, he breathed his last" (Lk 23:46 // Psa 31:5 NIV). This is a quotation of Psalm 31:5. Jesus prayed Scripture back to God. His prayer quoted Psalm 31:5.

Application:
Scripture that expresses our thoughts, needs, or emotions need to be prayed back to God.

Peter and John Acts 4:24-31 // Psalm 2:24-26

The prayer found in Acts 4:26 paraphrased the Scripture found in Psalm 2:1-2.

The back-story for the prayer: The followers of Jesus met together every day, praising God and enjoying the good will of all the people. Daily the Lord added to their number. At the temple gate, Peter and John healed a man born crippled, and then told the gathered crowd that the man was healed by the power of the name of Jesus. The religious leaders were upset because Peter and John proclaimed that dead people would come back to life through Jesus. They arrested Peter and John. The next day they questioned them. The religious leaders commanded Peter and John never to speak again in the name of Jesus (Ac 4:1-22).

The prayer: Peter and John returned to their group and they prayed, "Sovereign Lord, you made heaven, and earth, and the sea, and everything in them. King Herod, Pontius Pilate, with non-Jews and the Israelites conspired against your holy servant Jesus. What you have already planned, they made happen. Now, Lord, listen to their threats and help us, your servants, to speak your word with boldness. Stretch out your hand to heal and perform miracles through the name of your holy servant Jesus."

Peter and John prayed and their meeting place shook. All the gathered believers were filled with the Holy Spirit and they boldly spoke God's word (Ac 4:23-31).

Application:
When facing a problem, find Scripture that relates to the problem and pray it back to God.

Instead of asking God to remove a problem, ask God to help you deal with it. Peter and John did not ask God to protect them from the threats of violence made by the Jewish religious leaders, but to enable them to speak God's word with boldness (Ac 4:24-30).

WAYS TO PRAY THE SCRIPTURE

We can find guidelines in Scripture about how we should pray. The Bible tells us about God and Christ so that we can praise Him. It tells us about what God the Father, Jesus Christ, and the Holy

Spirit have done so that we can thank Him and express our faith. It tells us what God expects from us so that we can commit to obey and cry out for His help. It shows us how we failed to obey God so we can confess our sins. We need to learn to pray the Scripture. I'm including suggestions on different ways to pray the Scripture.

1. **Pray Scripture Prayers**

    Make prayers found in Scripture your prayers by either reading them back to God or rephrasing the prayers in your own words to God. Read the Scripture prayer as your own prayer. You may need to change some pronouns into personal pronouns.

    When we read prayers recorded in the Bible and we think about what we are reading, we are praying Scripture. If we pray those biblical prayers, we will find ourselves in agreement with the Spirit of God, and we will desire what God desires. Also, when we pray biblical prayers, we will not pray for our own agenda, nor the success of our own programs, nor for our political convictions to be established as the norm. Rather, we will focus on the establishment of God's rule and reign.

    We can find many prayers in the Bible that we can adapt and pray as our prayers. A great portion of the Psalms are prayers. Some of Jesus' prayers are recorded. Jesus gave His followers a model prayer to pray. Paul recorded numerous prayers that he prayed for the people that he wrote to.

- Examples of adapting Scripture prayers and making them my prayers:

    - Scripture: "But who can discern their own errors? Forgive my hidden faults. Keep your servant also from willful sins; may they not rule over me. Then I will be blameless, innocent of great transgression. May these words of my mouth and the meditation of my heart be pleasing in your sight, O Lord, my Rock and my Redeemer" (Psa 19:12-14 NIV).
    My Prayer: "Forgive me of my wrong-doings that I've hidden from others but you see. Keep me from intentionally committing sins that could become habits and then addictions. May both my spoken words that all can

hear, and my recurring thoughts that only you and I know about, be pleasing to you."

- Scripture: "And this is my prayer: that your love may abound more and more in knowledge and depth of insight, so that you may be able to discern what is best and may be pure and blameless for the day of Christ, filled with the fruit of righteousness that comes through Jesus Christ—to the glory and praise of God" (Phil 1:9-11 NIV).
My Prayer: "I pray for the church where I'm temporarily preaching until it finds a permanent pastor. I pray that the church members' love will keep on growing because of their biblical knowledge and insight. May they be able to discern what is best to know, think, and do. May they be pure and blameless until the day when Christ returns. May they experience Jesus Christ producing fruits of righteousness in their lives so they will bring glory and praise to God."

2. **Pray the Psalms**

Praying the Psalms is another approach to praise and worship God through His word. Psalms contain different types of prayers such as adoration, supplication, worship, praise, confession, and intercession.

Read the chosen Psalm out loud slowly and thoughtfully. Don't just read it; pray it to God. Then express your mental agreement to what the Psalm says. Seek to emotionally agree with the Psalm by expressing the same emotions the psalmist expressed.

Paraphrase the Psalm. Read the Psalm until you understand it enough to put it into your own words. Then pray your paraphrase to God.

- Examples of adapting a Psalm and making my prayers:
  - Scripture: "Blessed is the one who does not walk in step with the wicked or stand in the way that sinners take or sit in the company of mockers, but whose delight is in the law of the Lord, and who meditates on His law day and night. That person is like a tree planted by streams of water, which yields its fruit in season and whose leaf does not

wither—whatever they do prospers. Not so the wicked! They are like chaff that the wind blows away. Therefore the wicked will not stand in the judgment, nor sinners in the assembly of the righteous. For the Lord watches over the way of the righteous, but the way of the wicked leads to destruction" (Psa 1:1-6 NIV).

My Prayer: "My Father, I want to be blessed by you; therefore, I will not seek and follow the advice of wicked people, nor take the path of wrong-doing sinners, nor join in the social life of mockers. But I will delight in the teachings of your Bible and will intentionally think about your word. I trust that if I do those things, I will become as productive as a fruit-bearing tree planted beside a creek. Protect me from becoming a wicked person that is like husks that the wind blows away. I praise you, Father, because you know me and watch over the way I live."

3. **Pray the Way Jesus Taught Us to Pray**

The Lord's Prayer Matthew 6:9-13; Luke 11:2-4

"This, then, is how you should pray: 'Our Father in heaven, hallowed be your name, your kingdom come, your will be done, on earth as it is in heaven. Give us today our daily bread. And forgive us our debts, as we also have forgiven our debtors. And lead us not into temptation, but deliver us from the evil one'" (Mat 6:9-13).

This is commonly known as the Lord's Prayer; however, this is not a prayer Jesus prayed. It is a model prayer to teach His disciples guidelines on how to pray. Luke records Jesus teaching the prayer in response to the disciples' request for Jesus to teach them how to pray (Lk 11:1). The disciples did not ask Jesus to teach them a prayer. Jesus did not expect His disciples to constantly repeat the prayer. In fact, in Matthew 6:7, Jesus criticized vain repetition in prayer.

- The prayer is addressed to "Our Father in heaven" (Mat 6:9).
    - "Our" implies that the believer prays by virtue of his being a part of a community of believers.
    - "Father." Jesus addressed his personal prayers to the Father. Now, he teaches His disciples to address their

prayers to the same Father. The Aramaic word Jesus used for Father was "Abba," which can be translated "Daddy" or "Papa." The word denotes intimacy and respect.
- Six petitions that are expressed as urgent requests are included in the prayer (Mat 6:9-13).
    - 1st "Hallowed be your name" (Mat 6:9). This is an urgent request for God to cause His name to be hallowed. The verb hallowed means "to set apart" or "to sanctify." This is a request for God the Father to make His name special, above the ordinary, or honored.
    - 2nd "Your kingdom come" (Mat 6:10). This is an urgent request for God the Father to cause His kingdom to be established. It is a request for God's purposes in history to be completed.
    - 3rd "Your will be done, on earth as it is in heaven" (Mat 6:10). This urgent request explains what it will take for God's kingdom to come. When people on earth are doing God's will in the same way as angels in heaven, then God's kingdom will have arrived. The ultimate realization of this request will be answered when God's purposes in history are completely realized at the return of Christ to earth.

Petitions four through six are petitions of personal concerns. At this point, the prayer changes from petitions of aspiring to see God's purposes completed to petitions of personal concern.

- 4th "Give us today our daily bread" (Mat 6:11). Bread was a term that covered the idea of food. This is an urgent request for food needed for the immediate day. This is a prayer for immediate material need. (*This is the only instance in the New Testament where material needs are mentioned in connection with prayer.*)
- 5th "And forgive us our debts, as we also have forgiven our debtors" (Mat 6:12). This is an urgent petition for forgiveness. "Debts" refers to moral debts which believers incur with God when they violate His moral law. This is a model prayer for believers who know God as their Father. Therefore, it is a request for forgiveness for actions that hinder fellowship between the believer and the Father within God's family. "As we also have forgiven our debtors" implies that it is a forgiving person who seeks and receives

God's forgiveness. An unforgiving person is living in sin and does not receive God's forgiveness.

6th "And lead us not into temptation, but deliver us from the evil one" (Mat 6:13). The word "temptation" also means "testing." This is an urgent request for God to free us from falling into sin when experiencing temptation. "The evil one" is a reference to Satan who tempts people to sin. The believer who welcomes temptation is courting disaster.

Applications:
- We believers have an intimate child-parent relationship with God and are instructed to address the God of the universe as Father.
- Believers should pray with a sense of urgency. All the petitions were stated in the language of urgent request.
- Our prayers should be primary for spiritual needs. Five of the six petitions were for spiritual issues. We should pray with the realization that our real battles in life are in the realm of the spiritual rather than the material.
- The one request for daily bread teaches us that we need to bring immediate material needs to the Father in prayer. Material needs are important, but spiritual needs are most important.

Ask the Father for laborers to be sent into the harvest fields
Matthew 9:37-38

"So he (*Jesus*) said to his disciples, 'The harvest is large, but there are few workers to gather it in. Pray to the owner of the harvest that he will send out workers to gather in his harvest'" (Mat 9:37-38 NIV).

Jesus told the disciples to ask the owner of the harvest to send workers to harvest His crops. A waving field of golden wheat demands reapers and demands haste. When Jesus referred to the harvest, He meant that the multitude of people that flocked to His ministry was prepared to receive the gospel; but the workers were few. Therefore, Jesus directed His disciples to pray to the Lord of the harvest to send forth workers to harvest the crop. God is the owner of the great harvest of the world, and only He can send workers to gather it in.

Jesus wanted the disciples to start with prayer, but it did not end with prayer. Jesus called the disciples not only to pray but to be involved in being sent as well. Shortly after ordering His disciples to pray for the Lord to send workers to harvest His crops, Jesus gave His disciples authority (Mat 10:1) and He sent them out (Mat 10:5).

Jesus had already referred to people as a spiritual harvest. When He saw a crowd of Samaritans coming toward Him, Jesus saw them as fields white as for the spiritual harvest, and He spoke of him that sows seeds and him that harvests the crop (Jn 4:35-36).

Applications:

A group of people who have no biblical, spiritual instruction can be a plenteous spiritual harvest, and they need many active workers. Christ is the Lord of the harvest. We need to pray that many may be raised up and sent forth to work in bringing people to Christ.

When believers pray for workers in God's harvest, God will commission workers in answer to prayer, and God will bestow special mercy upon the people whom believers prayed to receive workers.

We who pray for workers in the Lord's harvest need to be willing to become the answer to our own prayers and to be sent out as workers by God.

Be persistent

Parable of the Friend at Midnight Luke 11:5-13

"Then Jesus said to them, 'Suppose you have a friend, and you go to him at midnight and say, 'Friend, lend me three loaves of bread; a friend of mine on a journey has come to me, and I have no food to offer him.' And suppose the one inside answers, 'Don't bother me. The door is already locked, and my children and I are in bed. I can't get up and give you anything.' I tell you, even though he will not get up and give you the bread because of friendship, yet because of your shameless audacity he will surely get up and give you as much as you need. So I say to you: Ask and it will be given to you; seek and you will find; knock and the door will be opened to you. For everyone who asks receives; the one who seeks finds; and to the one who knocks, the door will be opened. Which of you fathers, if your son asks for a fish, will give him a snake instead? Or if he asks for an egg, will give him a scorpion? If you then, though you are evil, know how to give good gifts to your children, how much more will your Father in heaven give the Holy Spirit to those who ask him!" (Lk 11:5-13).

Back-story:
Jesus was praying. When He stopped praying, one of His disciples asked Him to teach them to pray (Lk 11:1). The disciples noticed that something was special about the way Jesus prayed, and they wanted to know the secret. Jesus told them the Parable of the Friend at Midnight to teach them how prayer petitions are to be made.

Analysis of the parable:
- In the Jewish culture of Jesus' day, it was a disgrace not to offer a guest something to eat. The man in the parable faced a crisis, an embarrassing situation – a traveling friend stopped at his house and he had nothing to offer him to eat. He would have lost his honor and felt shame if he did not provide food for his guest. So the man did something that he would never have done under normal circumstances. He pounded on his neighbor's door at midnight. A crisis situation made the man aware of a great need.
- The man petitioned his friend with a specific request, three loaves of bread (Lk 11:5).
- He went directly to his friend. In the same way, we can go straight to our Father with our desires.
- Prayer petitions should include reasoning. The pleading man explained that a friend had arrived and he had no food to serve him.
- A great need gave the man shameless audacity. The desperation to preserve his reputation made him both bold and persistent. It was a shameless act to pound on the neighbor's door at midnight, and to keep on pounding after his friend refused his request. But the person who faces a crisis will be both shameless and persistent.

Analysis of Jesus' explanation of the parable:
- When experiencing a crisis, prayer becomes a time of desperate pleading. The verbs "ask," "seek," "knock" are in a tense that emphasize continuous action. Seek is more intense than asking, and knocking is more intense than seeking. The translated word for knocking was not a light tapping on the door but an insistent pounding (Lk 11:9).
- Tough, persistent prayer will get results. The one who asks and keeps asking will receive. The one who searches and keeps searching will find. And, the one who knocks and keeps knocking will experience an open door (Lk 11:10).
- God the Father will not deceive His children. An earthly father with many faults would not deceive his children by substituting something harmful, but similar in appearance to the object his child requested. If the child asked for a fish, the father would not deceive him by giving him a snake, or if the child asked for an egg, the father would not deceive him by giving him a scorpion.
- God the Father can be trusted. Earthly fathers who have many faults give good things to their children. Therefore, we can depend upon our perfect heavenly Father to give His children what is best for them.

Applications:
- When a crisis situation makes us aware of a great need, our reaction should be to pray.
- Our prayer request should be a specific request.
- We should be both bold and persistent in our prayers.
- Prayer can be work – hard work.
- Intense, persistent prayer gets results.
- We can trust God the Father not to deceive us, but to give us what is best for us.

Parable of the Unjust Judge Luke 18:1-8

"Then Jesus told his disciples a parable to show them that they should always pray and not give up. He said: 'In a certain town there was a judge who neither feared God nor cared what people thought. And there was a widow in that town who kept coming to him with the plea, 'Grant me justice against my adversary.' For some time he refused. But finally he said to himself, 'Even though I don't fear God or care what people think, yet because this widow keeps bothering me, I will see that she gets justice, so that she won't eventually come and attack me!' And the Lord said, 'Listen to what the unjust judge says. And will not God bring about justice for his chosen ones, who cry out to him day and night? Will he keep putting them off? I tell you, he will see that they get justice, and quickly. However, when the Son of Man comes, will he find faith on the earth?'" (Lk 18:1-8 NIV).

Analysis of the parable:
- The unfavorable character of the judge implies that no one could expect to receive any consideration from him. The judge neither feared God nor cared what the people thought (Lk 18:2).
- In Jesus' day, widows were helpless and had no influence. A helpless widow would have no hope of persuading an unscrupulous judge. The widow's only weapon was her persistence in continually pestering the judge (Lk 18:3).
- The judge changed his attitude toward the widow's request solely because of the woman's persistence (Lk 18:4-5).
- Jesus contrasted the unjust and selfish judge with the just and gracious God (Lk 18:7-8). God will respond to persistent prayer, more surely than the unjust judge.
- Jesus also drew attention to the one area where the unjust judge and God are similar – delay. During the time when God delays, God's chosen ones cry out to Him day and night (Lk 18:7).

Applications:
- When our prayers are unanswered, we are to persist in praying, in spite of the temptation to give up on God.
- When God delays to answer prayer petitions, and we feel like we are in God's waiting room, it is not because God is selfish or indifferent.
- God may delay answering our prayers; however, persistent continuous prayer will be answered.

Remain in Jesus, John 15:7

"If you remain in me and my words remain in you, ask whatever you wish, and it will be done for you" (Jn 15:7 NIV).

John 15:7 is in the context of John 15:1-8, where Jesus compares himself to being the Vine and His disciples being the branches. Jesus Christ is the true Vine. Believers are branches of the Vine: Jesus.

The verse has two halves, a condition and a result.

The condition establishes a state of affairs that must exist before something else will happen. The condition is the "if" clause: "If you remain in me and my words remain in you"(Jn 15:7). To remain in Christ is to stay connected to Him, the way branches are connected to a vine. This depicts a person who is wholly joined with Christ, totally submissive to Him, and totally dependent upon Him. When Christ's words remain in a person, that person will hold fast to Christ's teachings. He firmly believes Christ's declarations, obeys His commands, and relies on His promises.

The results establish the consequences of the condition being met. The results of the condition being met: "ask whatever you wish, and it will be done for you." People who meet the conditions will have their prayers heard and answered. The person who meets the conditions will make petitions that are according to God's will. (See 1 John 1:14-15.) Christ's indwelling words will result in the believer having such a harmony with Christ that his prayer request will be in harmony with God's divine will.

Applications:
- It is only when we keep Christ's commandments, when we live by faith in Him, and when His words control our conduct and affections, that our prayers will be heard.

Petition in Jesus' Name, John 14:12-14; 15:16; 16:23-24

"Very truly I tell you, whoever believes in me will do the works I have been doing, and they will do even greater things than these, because I am going to the Father. And I will do whatever you ask in my name, so that the Father may be glorified in the Son. You may ask me for anything in my name, and I will do it" (Jn 14:12-14 NIV).

"You did not choose me, but I chose you and appointed you so that you might go and bear fruit—fruit that will last—and so that whatever you ask in my name the Father will give you" (Jn 15:16 NIV).

"In that day you will no longer ask me anything. Very truly I tell you, my Father will give you whatever you ask in my name. Until now you have not asked for anything in my name. Ask and you will receive, and your joy will be complete" (Jn 16:23-24 NIV).

Commentary:
- The New Testament speaks of doing several things in Jesus' Name:
  - Gathering together in Jesus' name (Mat 18:20)
  - Welcoming a child in Jesus' name (Mk 9:37)
  - Giving a cup of water in Jesus' name (Mk 9:41)
  - All who believe in Jesus' name become children of God (Jn 1:12)
  - Those who believe that Jesus is the Christ, the Son of God, have life in Jesus' name (Jn 20:31)

- What it means to pray in Jesus' Name:
  - To represent Jesus when we speak to God in prayer. In the Bible, to do something in the "name" of God, or of an individual, meant to act in accordance with that person's character. It meant to act or speak just as that person would, and to do it in such a way that honors the reputation of that person. To pray in Jesus' name means that we pray just as if Jesus were praying, and we pray in a way that brings honor to Jesus. We identify ourselves with Jesus and pray seeking the things He would seek. To pray as Jesus' representative means that I come asking for Jesus' will to be accomplished and for His name or glory to be honored.
  - To recognize that we do not deserve the right to pray to God. Jesus gives us the right to enter into God's presence using His name, when we could never come before God because of who we are.
  - Our position before God rests in Jesus Christ, and we pray in the name of Jesus so that God the Father will hear our prayers. People become the children of God and are brought into a personal relationship with God through faith in Jesus. Believers' relationship with Jesus and their being

in Jesus allows them the privilege of coming into God's presence through prayer, and of being heard.

Applications:
Praying in Jesus' name means that we approach the Father in prayer, seeking only what Jesus would seek, and seeking what would honor His reputation and purposes in this world.

Some misapply this verse, claiming that praying "in Jesus' name" at the end of a prayer results in God's always granting what is asked for. This treats the words "in Jesus' name" as a magic formula, and treats God like a mystical genie or Santa Claus—as though He exists only to fulfill our requests. If our prayer requests are not for God's glory and according to His will, saying "in Jesus' name" at the end of a prayer is not a magic formula. Genuinely praying in Jesus' name and for His glory is what is important, not attaching certain words to the end of a prayer. It is not the words in the prayer that matter, but the purpose behind the prayer.

I lived in Brasilia, Brazil for thirteen years. On one occasion, I was unsuccessful in getting an appointment with the director of a certain hospital. I mentioned my frustration to a church member whose brother-in-law was a cabinet official to the president. A couple of hours later, the church member called me and told me to go to the hospital and to request an appointment with the hospital director, saying I was coming in the name of the cabinet official. I could not get an appointment with the hospital director using my own name, but when I said the cabinet official told me to come in his name, I was attended. In the same way, God will not listen to my prayers when I come in my own name, but Jesus has given me the privilege of using His name to gain the Father's attention.

4. **Pray the Way Paul Taught Us to Pray**

Acts 9:11
"The Lord told him, 'Go to the house of Judas on Straight Street and ask for a man from Tarsus named Saul, for he is praying'" (Ac 9:11 NIV).

Back-story:
Stephen was one of the seven men chosen to help the apostles distribute food to the widows. Men falsely accused Stephen,

arrested him, and stoned him to death. Saul approved Stephen's stoning. Saul went from house to house, arresting people who professed belief in Jesus. Saul received letters from the high priest that gave him permission to arrest anyone in Damascus who belonged to the Way of Christ.

Saul neared Damascus; a light from heaven flashed around him. Saul fell to the ground and heard a voice saying, "Saul, Saul, why do you persecute me?" Saul asked, "Who are you, Lord?" The voice answered, "I am Jesus, the one you're persecuting. Get up! Go into the city. You'll be told what you must do." Saul was blind. Saul's companions led him by the hand into Damascus. For three days Saul didn't eat nor drink (Ac 9:1-9). A believer named Ananias lived in Damascus. In a vision, the Lord told him to go to Saul, for he was praying.

Saul was a Pharisee. As a Pharisee, he was required to pray at least three times a day. Saul as a Pharisee had often said his prayers, yet he had never prayed. He merely went through the ritual and repeated formal prayers. But now the proud Pharisee, the unmerciful oppressor of the church was praying. Prior to this event, Saul breathed out threats and slaughter against the disciples of Christ; now he was breathing out communion with Christ.

Applications:
A person can routinely go through the ritual and say formal prayers without praying.
True prayer is a conversation with God.

Romans 8:26
"In the same way, the Spirit helps us in our weakness. We do not know what we ought to pray for, but the Spirit himself intercedes for us through wordless groans (Rom 8:26 NIV).

Commentary:
When believers fail to know God's will and consequently don't know how to specifically petition God, the Holy Spirit intervenes, and He expresses to God the Father those intercessory petitions that perfectly match the will of God. When we do not know what to pray for, or when we pray for things that are not best for us, the Holy Spirit intercedes on our behalf.

When words can't express a person's deepest emotions, inarticulate wordless groans can be self-revealing. Grief communicates more in a sob and a tear than in spoken words. Love shouts with the light of an eye and the clasp of a hand. When groanings felt in the depths of the believer's soul can't be expressed by spoken words, the Holy Spirit interprets them and expresses those feelings and emotions to the Father. When the believer's prayers are too deep and too intense for words, when they are only a sigh or a groan heaved from the heart rather than any spoken words, then the Holy Spirit interprets and translates them into our prayers to God the Father.

When believers don't know what to pray for, the Holy Spirit renders us aid and takes our prayer request to the Father in a way that matches the will of the Father. Some reasons why believers don't know what to pray for:
- We don't know what is best for us.
- We don't know our own real needs.
- We don't know what God is wanting to do with us, our church, or our organization.
- We don't know what God desires to grant us.
- We may feel perplexed because of trouble, sickness, trials, temptations, calamities, or situations in life.
- We don't understand the character of God and the way He acts.
- Our spiritual vision is dim.

Paul included himself as one who didn't know what to pray for when he said the Spirit helps "us" in "our" weakness (Rom 8:26). Paul is an example of someone who didn't know what he should pray for. On three occasions, Paul prayed to be delivered from the thorn in the flesh (2 Cor 12:8-9). God didn't intend for Paul to be healed but God gave Paul grace sufficient to deal with his physical affliction (2 Cor 12:9-10).

Application:
Because we believers don't know what we should pray for as we ought, we could make endless mistakes in our prayers. The Holy Spirit prevents this from happening by reinterpreting our prayers to make them in line with God's will before presenting them to the Father.

Paul included himself as one who didn't know what to pray for when he said the Spirit helps "us" in "our" weakness (Rom 8:26). If Paul admitted he didn't know how to pray, we should not be surprised that we have the same problem.

Even though we don't know how to pray as we should, we should keep praying.

We Christians can be assured of God's protective guidance in spite of our often being unaware of what we should be doing, where we should be going, or what we should pray for.

As I was writing this, I didn't know how to pray for my wife who was struggling with a terminal illness. The doctor had given us bad news and he had tears in his eyes when he said, "I'm so sorry." Then he warned us that crises would become more frequent and pain more intense. I paid a high price for the privilege of caring for the one I loved when she was slowly moving toward death. It was hard to see my wife in constant pain and to know the pain could only be relieved by her death. I didn't want to see my wife suffer, but I didn't want to live without my beloved wife of fifty-two years. It was hard to observe her once brilliant mind become so confused that at times she didn't know my name. I didn't know how long to allow medical science to fight for her life, and when it would become cruel to allow procedures and medicine to prolong her life. How could I make that decision which would rip my heart from my chest? I didn't know when I should stop the nurses from giving her the medicine that was prolonging her suffering and giving her mental confusion. I didn't know how to pray, but I talked to God about my wife and my confusion, and I trusted the Holy Spirit to restate my prayers to the Father in a way that was according to His will.

My friend, John Ramsey, described his prayer life after the sudden and unexpected death of his wife Cami. John said, "With Cami's death, everything went dark. I literally felt like I had been hit by a Mack truck. My prayers were mostly sobbing as I kneeled beside our bed."

Because of Romans 8:6, I'm convinced that the Holy Spirit reinterpreted John's sobs and turned them into prayers that were presented to God the Father.

Philippians 4:6-7

"Do not be anxious about anything, but in every situation, by prayer and petition, with thanksgiving, present your requests to God. And the peace of God, which transcends all understanding, will guard your hearts and your minds in Christ Jesus" (Phil 4:6-7 NIV).

Commentary:

Paul advised us to not worry about anything; instead, pray about everything. When praying, we should both tell God our needs and thank Him. The consequences of following this orientation is that we will experience God's peace.

- Command: Do not worry about anything

Paul's command to not worry about anything echoes Jesus' teaching to not worry (Mat 6:25-34). Peter gave the advice to turn all our anxiety over to God because He cares for us (1 Pet 5:7).

Paul wrote Philippians while he was in prison. Paul found peace while in prison through prayer and thanksgiving; therefore, he spoke with experience and had authority to give this orientation.

Paul didn't just write, "Do not worry," but rather wrote, "Do not be worried about anything." Then he offered definite steps for experiencing peace instead of anxiety.

- Prescription for combating anxiety: Pray and give thanks

Paul wrote that to combat anxiety, pray about everything, no exceptions. In other words, every problem, every circumstance, every relationship, and every situation should be brought before the Father in prayer. Don't attempt to hide anything from God.

Two elements should be included in prayer:
- Petition. Petition is asking or making requests to God. And we should make specific requests to God.
- Thanksgiving. Prayer should reflect gratitude toward God for what He has done, for what He is doing, and for what He has given us. Thankfulness puts our thoughts on God, rather than on our problems. The demanding ungrateful person acts like God owes him. The grateful person takes the servant position of one who is indebted to God.

- The promise for those who follow the prescription:

Paul promised that if we stop worrying and instead tell God what we need and thank Him for what He has done, then we will experience God's peace. God's peace goes beyond anything we can imagine or what medical science can produce.

Paul did not promise that our problems would not get worse or that they would go away or we would understand our circumstances. Paul promised that fretting, worrying, and anxiety would be replaced with peace.

This peace passes all understanding; no one can explain it; neither can medical science duplicate it.

Application:

Scripture calls worry a sin. It is a sin in the same way that adultery or murder or theft is sin. When our stomachs are tied in knots because of worry and we are in a nervous frenzy, we have fallen into sin. Worry is similar to wearing a groove in the mud with our car tires. The more we spin our tires, the deeper and slicker the rut becomes.

Everything, every case, every situation, and every relationship should be brought to God by prayer, whether it be temporal or spiritual, relating to body or soul, to ourselves or others, to our families, relations, acquaintances, our church, or the world. This may include different sorts of prayer, mental or vocal, private or public, ordinary or extraordinary.

God deserves our praise and thankfulness.

When you find yourself worrying, you need to:
- Repent – confess that you are living as if God doesn't care or He is incapable of helping you.
- Pray – make your requests known to God.
- Give thanks – thank Him for His faithfulness in the past, for what He is doing for you in the present, for His willingness to help, and for His wisdom and grace.

1 Thessalonians 5:17

"Pray continually, give thanks in all circumstances; for this is God's will for you in Christ Jesus" (1 Thess 5:17 NIV).

Commentary:

The word translated "continually," was used of a hacking cough. The person with a hacking cough doesn't cough continually, but often and repeatedly. The word was also used of repeated military attacks. An army would attack a city, but not conquer it. The army would regroup and attack the city over and over until they conquered it. Believers should pray frequently and persistently. Believers who are dependent on God, and who realize that without Him they can do nothing, will always be in a spirit of prayer.

Believers should not only pray to God, they should also give constant thanks to Him. Indeed, the major portion of their prayers should be thanksgiving. Giving thanks in every situation doesn't mean that believers must be happy with every situation or become resigned to accept matters without praying and working for change. Give thanks in every circumstance – in joy and in sorrow, in prosperity and in poverty, in good times and in adversity, or when healthy and when sick. Believers should thank God in every place – at home or in the house of God, at work or on the bed of sickness. They can always find something to be thankful for, even for those dark and difficult circumstances.

Application:

The words, "pray continually," oppose the practice of those who pray not at all, or, having prayed, have stopped praying, or who only pray in a time of trouble and distress. The reason for praying with frequency and constancy is because we are always needy and we are always needing God's mercies.

Christians should not allow anything to stop them from praying. Some stop praying after a tragedy because they feel that God failed to protect them. Some stop praying after they sinned because they feel unworthy to enter God's presence. Some stop praying because they are discouraged. Some stop praying because they were betrayed by professing Christians. Some stop praying when God did not answer their prayers the way they requested; they feel that prayers are ineffective. Others stop praying when everything is going well because they feel they don't need God. Some feel they are too busy to take time to pray. Believers should never allow anything to stop them from praying.

We are to observe the duty of prayer in the closet, in the family, when alone, when with others, and at church services. We are not to allow our duty to pray to be interrupted by any cause.

We are to pray regularly, and when we pray we are to express thanks to God.

We don't need to feel thankful before we give thanks. When God takes us through hard trials, we don't feel thankful. But we can find reason to give thanks. Giving thanks in everything is often a choice to believe God in difficult circumstances.

I am not thankful that my wife has declining health and is experiencing constant pain, but I can find things to be thankful for. I am thankful that she has doctors who are interested in her as a person. I am thankful for each act of kindness nurses and other hospital staff show to her. I am thankful for the support of our three sons, our daughters-in-law, and our grandchildren.

1 Timothy 2:1-4

"I urge, then, first of all, that petitions, prayers, intercession and thanksgiving be made for all people – for kings and all those in authority, that we may live peaceful and quiet lives in all godliness and holiness. This is good, and pleases God our Savior, who wants all people to be saved and to come to a knowledge of the truth" (1 Tim 2:1-4 NIV).

Commentary:

In 1 Timothy 1, Paul gave Timothy the assignment, at the church at Ephesus, to correct teaching which had drifted from apostolic revelation into controversial areas that were destructive to faith. In chapter 2, Timothy's second assignment was to set in order the public worship of the assembly in Ephesus. In verses 1-4, he talks about public prayer.

- Paul lists four types of prayer:
  - Request. This refers to petitions for things that people want. It also implies requests for people where other people can get involved. If we are praying for somebody who does not have food, we can get involved and buy them groceries.

- Prayer. The word "prayer" sounds so generic in the English translation that it does little to clarify what Paul was saying. The Greek word Paul used in his writing referred to requests which God alone can meet. If someone is heartbroken, betrayed, or suffering from a tragedy that he does not understand and no one can explain – only God can meet that need.
- Intercession. The Greek word Paul used would refer to a petition made by a friend to a king on behalf of someone else. This is a type of prayer where we come to our heavenly Father and share with Him special needs and problems that others have. The needs of others should find a place in our prayer to God.
- Thanksgiving. Giving thanks to God for what He has done, is doing, and what He has given us.
- Paul lists the objects of prayer, telling us who we should pray for:
  - Everyone. We are to be ready and willing to pray for anyone, all people.
  - For kings and all in authority. Paul wrote these words when the emperor was Nero, one of the cruelest of Roman emperors. Nero launched a persecution against Christians. Yet, Paul wrote not to forget to pray for the king and all in authority. This would have included Emperor Nero. We need to pray for our leaders. They may be ungodly and cruel men, but, still, we are to pray for them.
- Paul lists the objective of prayer:
  - That we may live peaceful and quiet lives in all godliness and holiness. Paul implies that there is a relationship between prayer and peace. Christians being faithful in prayer for government leaders, results in citizens leading peaceful and quiet lives.
  - Prayer accomplishes the will of God who desires for everyone to be saved and to come to the knowledge of the truth. Paul implied that the prayerful life is good and acceptable to God because it is God's way of opening up people everywhere for salvation.

Application:
We are to pray for everyone with the different types of prayer. Everyone needs our prayer, and we will never meet someone that we can't or should not pray for.

We should pray that government leaders would govern so that we might enjoy a tranquil and quiet life. But the purpose for such a life is not that we might be comfortable and happy. We should pray for political peace so that we believers can live an observable godly life and freely tell others about Jesus, so non-believers will believe in Jesus and be saved.

Prayer is the first weapon that opens up a territory to possess it for God. When we pray for non-believers, we can expect that they will hear and understand truth that they have never heard nor understood before.

Paul's Prayer Request for Himself

Romans 15:30–33
"I urge you, brothers, by our Lord Jesus Christ and by the love of the Spirit, to join me in my struggle by praying to God for me. Pray that I may be rescued from the unbelievers in Judea and that my service in Jerusalem may be acceptable to the saints there, so that by God's will I may come to you with joy and together with you be refreshed. The God of peace be with you all. Amen" (Rom 15:30–33 NIV).

Back-story:
Paul informed the church at Rome of his plans to visit the church there when he traveled to Spain. But first, Paul was going to Jerusalem to take the love offering from the non-Jewish Christians to the Jerusalem church (Rom 15:23-29). Jews in Jerusalem were enraged against Paul on account of his preaching to non-Jews, and not requiring non-Jewish believers to obey the Mosaic Law. Jewish believers gave importance to the Mosaic Law, and they could not understand how Paul neglected and discouraged the observance of it among non-Jewish believers.

Commentary:
- Reasons Paul gave for urging the Christians in Rome to pray for him:

- For the Lord Jesus Christ (Rom 15:30). If not for Paul's sake, for the sake of the Lord Jesus Christ.
- For the love of the Spirit (Rom 15:30). They received love from the Spirit, and Paul wanted them to manifest that love by praying for him.
- Join Paul in his struggle by praying for him (Rom 15:30). Paul prayed for himself, but he desired that others join him in praying for him. The word "struggle" denoted intense effort, such as was used by wrestlers in the Greek games. Paul wanted them to make an intense effort in their prayers. Paul understood prayer as an agony, a holy conflict, and striving with God.

- Petitions Paul urges them to make to God on his behalf:
  - That he may be rescued from the unbelievers in Judea (Rom 15:31). Unbelieving Jews at Jerusalem knew that Paul preached salvation to non-Jews without requiring them to obey the law of Moses. And they falsely believed that Paul taught Jews who lived among non-Jews to forsake the Mosaic Law. Paul wanted prayers that he be protected from those enemies of Christ and Christ's servants.
  - That God's people in Jerusalem would accept the financial help he would bring to them (Rom 15:31). Knowing that the Jewish believers in Jerusalem had heard false accusations against him, Paul wanted prayers that they would receive the collections brought from non-Jewish believers.
  - That it would be God's will for Paul to go to Rome with joy, and both the Christians in Rome and Paul would be refreshed by his visit (Rom 15:32). Paul wanted prayers that his ministry would be acceptable to the believers in Rome and that it would bring a mutual benefit to both him and them. The refreshment Paul envisioned stems from the fellowship and joy that exists when members of the church mutually minister to one another.

God answered Paul's prayer request differently than he asked. Paul was rescued from the unbelieving Jews in Jerusalem, but only because Roman soldiers arrested him. Paul was sent to Rome as a prisoner. He was under house arrest in Rome and couldn't visit and minister to the church there. Acts chapters 21 through 28 tell the story of Paul's arrest and trip to Rome.

Application:
People who beg others to pray for them must also pray for themselves.

God made the accomplishment of His purposes depend on the preaching of His Word. And God made the success of preaching depend on prayer. God's goal to be glorified will only succeed with the proclamation of the gospel. And that gospel will only be proclaimed in power with the prevailing, earnest, faith-filled prayers of God's people.

Paul wanted believers to work at prayer, like wrestlers struggle to win a match. Sometimes praying is an enjoyable relaxed conversation with God; but at other times, we need to struggle, putting forth the effort similar to that of wrestlers in fierce combat. Such prayers are hard work. When it is hard to pray, we need to pray hard.

We don't wrestle with God in prayer. We can't arm-wrestle God because we couldn't win; and also, God knows what is best for us. But at times, intense prayers require us to put forth as much effort as an athlete who is competing in a wrestling match.

Believers everywhere should put forth great effort in prayer for the preachers/teachers of the gospel – pray that they would be kept from temptation and that they would be protected from dangerous attacks from non-believers.

Some missionaries go to people groups who torture, imprison, or kill Christians. We especially need to pray for missionaries who proclaim the gospel to people who are hostile toward it.

We need to make our plans subordinate to the will of God and adapt to His will when it is different from our plans.

Paul's request for prayer while a prisoner Ephesians 6:19–20; Colossians 4:2–4

"Pray also for me, that whenever I open my mouth, words may be given me so that I will fearlessly make known the mystery of the gospel, for which I am an ambassador in chains. Pray that I may declare it fearlessly, as I should" (Eph 6:19–20 NIV).

"Devote yourselves to prayer, being watchful and thankful. And pray for us, too, that God may open a door for our message, so that we may proclaim the mystery of Christ, for which I am in chains. Pray that I may proclaim it clearly, as I should" (Col 4:2–4 NIV).

Back-story:
Paul penned the letters to the Ephesians and the Colossians when he was a prisoner (Eph 3:1; 4:1; 6:20; Col 4:3). Disagreement exists concerning whether Paul was imprisoned in Caesarea (Ac 24:22) around A.D. 57-59 or in Rome (Ac 28:30) around A.D 60-62. Ephesians and Colossians are two of the four epistles commonly known as the Prison Epistles. The others are Philippians and Philemon.

Commentary:
Paul constantly prayed for others, and he also earnestly requested that others should constantly pray for him.
- Paul's prayer requests:
  - That God would open a door for his message (Col 4:3). He wanted God to give him an opportunity to speak about Christ.
  - That when he spoke, the right words would be given to him (Eph 6:19) so that he might speak clearly (Col 4:4).
  - That he would boldly reveal the mystery of the gospel (Eph 6:19, 20). That he would speak boldly when he spoke about the good news of Jesus to people who did not understand it.
- The reason for his prayer requests:
  - Paul was an ambassador for Christ in chains. He was Christ's representative, but he was a prisoner (Eph 6:20; Col 3:3).

Paul was in prison with criminals, and he was guarded by non-believing soldiers when he wrote his Prison Epistles. But Paul did not ask the church to pray for the salvation of sinful criminals and soldiers. Paul asked the church to pray for him that God would give him an opportunity to speak about Christ, that Paul would have the right words to say, and he would have the courage to say them.

Application:
Spiritual leaders such as preachers and Bible teachers need to pray for others. They also need the prayers of fellow Christians. No leader is perfect in this life, and those who are more visible need the prayers of those who are less visible.

God made the salvation of non-believers depend on believers telling non-believers about Jesus. And God made the success of telling people about Jesus depend on prayer. The gospel's good news will only be proclaimed in power with the prevailing, earnest, faith-filled prayers of God's people.

God desires that non-believers become believers and be saved from their sins. If we imitate Paul when we are concerned about the salvation of non-believers, our prayer emphasis will not be for the salvation of non-believers; our prayer emphasis will be for believers who have contact with non-believers. We will pray in the following manner:

- That God gives us believers relationships with non-believers.
- That God would open the door to give us believers opportunities to communicate God's message to non-believers.
- That when God opens the door for us to tell non-believers about Jesus, we would have the right words to say.
- That when God opens the door for us to tell non-believers about Jesus and gives us the right words, we would have the courage to say them.

2 Thessalonians 3:1-2

"As for other matters, brothers and sisters, pray for us that the message of the Lord may spread rapidly and be honored, just as it was with you. And pray that we may be delivered from wicked and evil people, for not everyone has faith" (2 Thess 3:1-2 NIV).

Commentary:
The Christian leader's power can increase as time passes from the accumulation of prayers from his spiritual children. Paul prayed for the believers he had evangelized; he also asked them to pray for him. Paul left people praying for him everywhere (Rom 15:30; 2 Cor 1:11; Eph 6:18-19; Col 4:3; 1Thes 5:25). Paul's main prayer request

was for help in his work of evangelizing, not for protection from pain and danger.

- Paul asked for prayer in two categories:
  - That the gospel might advance in two ways:
    (1) <u>That the Lord's message may spread rapidly</u>. This is a prayer that the word of the Lord would advance unhindered and without obstacles.
    (2) <u>That the gospel might be honored</u> (2 Thess 3:1). Paul's prayer request alluded to the gospel as a runner in the Olympic Games. The gospel was already on the race track. May it meet no obstruction and run its course, so it might get to the goal, and be glorified by gaining the crown appointed for the runner who gets first to the finish line.
  - That Paul and his co-workers would be delivered from wicked and evil people (2 Thess 3:2). Paul was in Corinth when he wrote to the Thessalonians. Acts 18:6, 9, and 12 describe the evil people who opposed him there. Paul was probably referring to two groups who opposed the gospel.
    (1) <u>Unbelieving Jewish zealots</u>, who opposed him for preaching salvation to non-Jews, without requiring them to obey the Law of Moses. They followed him from place to place, always raising a persecution against him.
    (2) <u>Greek philosophers</u> who boasted of being lovers of wisdom and possessing truth. When Paul said, "not everyone has faith," he probably referred to teachers, both Jewish and non-Jewish, who became unreasonable and wicked even though they professed faith in the truth.

Believers who pray for their preachers/teachers, assist them and help them succeed. Prayer and preaching are different, yet go hand in hand. Prayer speaks to God for people; preaching speaks to people for God. Prayer seeks to bring God to people; preaching seeks to bring people to God. Prayer tells God what people want; preaching tells people what God wants them to do. Preaching sows the seed; prayer brings the rain and the sunshine that causes the seed to grow.

Paul and his team recognized their own inadequacy and their need of God's enablement, and they humbly sought prayer support from others.

Satan is ineffective against God's word when it is accurately proclaimed. Satan may deny it, attack it, try to add to it or subtract from it, but his primary attacks are against those who proclaim it. Satan seeks to use those who do not have faith in Jesus and who are under his influence to tempt, deceive, accuse, imprison, distract, detain, kill, or in some way negate the testimony of the messenger.

Application:
Paul requested his spiritual children to pray for him and his team. God made the success of His gospel dependent, in a certain measure, on the prayers of us believers. The progress of the gospel is not to be attributed to the power of the preacher, but to the power of God in answer to prayer.

If Paul, with all his supernatural endowments, required the prayers of God's people, how much more will ordinary preachers and small group Bible teachers.

Believers who are separated by distance may join together in prayer.

God's word will not return empty; it will accomplish what God desires (Is 55:11). God's word is effective when we communicate it to those without Christ, but it is not effective if we do not share it. Seeds must be sown if a harvest is to be reaped. How frequently we share the gospel determines if it walks or runs. It is one thing for the gospel to walk and it is another for it to run. We should each have a burden to spread the gospel frequently and help it run.

Enemies to the gospel, who show malice and persecute its faithful preachers, are unreasonable and wicked.

Those who most opposed Paul were religious Jewish zealots who did not have faith in Jesus Christ. Fierce opposition to the true preaching of God's word often comes from religious people who profess to believe in God but who neither believe nor practice what the Bible teaches.

5. **Pray God's Promises**
The *DICTIONARY OF BIBLE THEMES* discovered 5,467 of God's promises in the Bible.

- The Bible affirms that God keeps His promises. Believers in Christ can depend on God to keep His promises. But we need to remember that many promises are conditional upon believers obeying God's commands. We need to believe that God will do what He promised in the Scripture.
  - When Joshua was an old man he said, "Now I am about to go the way of all the earth. You know with all your heart and soul that not one of all the good promises the Lord your God gave you has failed. Every promise has been fulfilled; not one has failed" (Jos 23:14 NIV).
  - The Apostle Paul said, "For no matter how many promises God has made, they are "Yes" in Christ. And so through him the 'Amen' is spoken by us to the glory of God (2 Cor 1:20 NIV).
  - The Apostle Peter said, "Through these he has given us his very great and precious promises, so that through them you may participate in the divine nature, having escaped the corruption in the world caused by evil desires" (2 Pet 1:4 NIV).

Pray back the Holy Spirit's inspired promises made by God by reading out loud His promises and telling Him we believe them. This will help us understand God's plans and agenda and for our desires to fall in line with His. Praying God's promises will help you pray with wisdom and authority.

- Here are some Bible promises, but there are many more:
  - <u>Eternal life</u>. "And this is what he promised us—eternal life" (1 Jn 2:25 NIV).
  - <u>God can do the impossible</u>. "What is impossible with man is possible with God" (Lk 18:27 NIV).
  - <u>God's plans are for our own good</u>. "'For I know the plans I have for you,' declares the Lord, 'plans to prosper you and not to harm you, plans to give you hope and a future'" (Jer 29:11NIV).
  - <u>God gives power to the weak and powerless</u>. "He gives strength to the weary and increases the power of the weak. Even youths grow tired and weary, and young men stumble and fall; but those who hope in the Lord will renew their strength. They will soar on wings like eagles; they will

run and not grow weary, they will walk and not be faint" (Is 40:29-31 NIV).
- God will supply our needs. "And my God will meet all your needs according to the riches of his glory in Christ Jesus" (Phil 4:19 NIV).
- Nothing can separate us from God's love. "No, in all these things we are more than conquerors through him who loved us. For I am convinced that neither death nor life, neither angels nor demons, neither the present nor the future, nor any powers, neither height nor depth, nor anything else in all creation, will be able to separate us from the love of God that is in Christ Jesus our Lord" (Rom 8:37-39 NIV).
- Believers in Christ will be saved. "If you declare with your mouth, 'Jesus is Lord,' and believe in your heart that God raised him from the dead, you will be saved" (Rom 10:9 NIV).
- The Holy Spirit's power to tell others about Jesus. Jesus said, "But you will receive power when the Holy Spirit comes on you; and you will be my witnesses in Jerusalem, and in all Judea and Samaria, and to the ends of the earth" (Ac 1:8 NIV).
- Believers will do greater works than Jesus did. Jesus said, "Very truly I tell you, whoever believes in me will do the works I have been doing, and they will do even greater things than these, because I am going to the Father" (Jn 14:12 NIV).
- Prayers asked in Jesus' name will be answered. Jesus said, "And I will do whatever you ask in my name, so that the Father may be glorified in the Son. You may ask me for anything in my name, and I will do it" (Jn 14:13-14 NIV).
- Jesus' followers will experience peace. Jesus promised, "Peace I leave with you; my peace I give you. I do not give to you as the world gives. Do not let your hearts be troubled and do not be afraid" (Jn 14:27 NIV).
- Believers can stand against the devil's schemes. "Put on the full armor of God, so that you can take your stand against the devil's schemes" (Eph 6:11 NIV).

6. **Pray to Commit to Obey Bible Commands**
Biblical promises should be believed; biblical commands should be obeyed. Many Old Testament commandments are not directly binding for Christians. Nonetheless, keeping the Ten Commandments and other Old Testament moral commands remain imperative. New Testament commands, given by Jesus and the apostles, set out the commands of God and Jesus Christ for believers.

Prophet Samuel told King Saul that to obey is better than sacrifice and that rejecting the word of God results in being rejected by God (1 Sam 15:22-23).

Jesus illustrated with the parable of the House Built on the Rock and the House Built on the Sand as being the difference between those who obey Him and those who disobey Him. People who hear Jesus' words and put them into practice are like the wise man who built his house on the rock. People who do not put them into practice are like the foolish man who built his house on the sand (Mat 7:24-27).

Jesus taught that to love Him was to obey His commands (Jn 14:15; 15:10-17).

The Apostle John taught that to love God is to obey God's commands (1 Jn 5:2-3).

- Here are some Bible commands, but there are many more:

<u>Short Form of the Ten Commandments</u> (Ex 20:1-17):
- Do not have any other gods before me.
- Do not make idols.
- Do not take the name of the Lord your God in vain.
- Remember the Sabbath day, to keep it holy.
- Honor your father and your mother.
- Do not murder.
- Do not commit adultery.
- Do not steal.
- Do not bear false witness against your neighbor.
- Do not covet.

<u>Jesus' summary of the most important commandments:</u>
- Love God with our heart, soul, mind, and strength and your neighbors as yourselves (Mk 12:29–31).

Some commands of Jesus:

- Repent (Mat 4:17; Lk 13:3).
- Let not your heart be troubled (Jn 14:27; 16:33; Mat 6:25-26).
- Let your light shine (Mat 5:14-16).
- Be reconciled with your brother or sister who has something against you (Mat 5:23-24).
- Keep your word (Mat 5:33-37).
- Love your enemies (Mat 5:44).
- Lay up treasures in heaven (Mat 6:19-21).
- Seek first the kingdom of God (Mat 6:33).
- Judge not (Mat 7:1-2).
- Do not throw your pearls to pigs (Mat 7:6).
- Do to others as you would have them do to you (Mat 7:12).
- Beware of false prophets (Mat 7:15).
- Pray for the Father to send workers into His harvest field (Mat 9:37-38).
- Fear God, but do not fear people (Mat 10:28;. Lk 12:4-5).
- Listen to God's voice (Mat 11:15, 13:9).
- Honor your parents (Mat 15:4).
- Beware of false teaching (Mat 16:6, 11-12).
- Do not despise little ones (Mat 18:10).
- Go to the fellow believer who offended you (Mat 18:15 // Gal 6:1).
- Forgive people who offended you (Mat 18:21-22 // Pro 19:11).
- Beware of covetousness (Lk 12:15).
- Honor marriage (Mat 19:6, 9).
- Lead by being a servant (Mat 20:26-28).
- Pray in faith (Mat 21:21-22, Jn 15:7).
- Give to Caesar what belongs to him (*pay the taxes that the government requires*) (Mat 22:19-21).
- Love the Lord (Mat 22:37-38).
- Love your neighbor as you love yourself (Mat 22:39).
- Await the return of Jesus (Mat 24:42-44).
- Celebrate the Lord's supper (Mat 26:26-27).
- Watch and pray (Mat 26:41).
- Keep Jesus' commandments (Jn 14:15).
- Make and baptize disciples, and teach them to obey Jesus (Mat 28:19-20).

Pray back the Holy Spirit's inspired commands. Commit yourself to obey them, and ask God to help you keep your commitment. You will be committing yourself to a life which reflects your love for Christ and building your life on the foundation that pleases God.

7. **Read the Bible to God as a Part of Your Prayer**
When we read the Bible during our prayers to God, we are reminding God of His word. God doesn't need the reminder, but He loves to see that we are reading and learning His word.

8. **Talk to God about a Scripture Text**
After reading the Bible, talk to God about what He said to you during the reading of His word.

- Suggestions for talking to God about His word:
  • Tell God how you are applying His word to your life

I started writing this part on Friday, 3:30 a.m. My wife entered a hospice facility on Wednesday. The hospice nurse told me that my wife showed the signs of having only a few hours to live on this earth. But she had continued to struggle to breathe for over forty hours. I was unable to sleep; I read Psalm 46:1-2.

"God is our refuge and strength, an ever-present help in trouble. Therefore we will not fear" (Psa 46:1-2 NIV).

After reading the psalmist's words, I talked to God about what I read. I said, "God, I believe the psalmist was comparing you to a walled city. When an enemy army threatened to invade the country, the rural people fled to the city as a place of refuge. When my wife began to suffer declining health, we together sought refuge in you.

"The walled city was a place of strength during a battle. It was a stronghold, a fortress, and those inside the fortress had an advantage over those outside. Those outside the wall were exposed because all bushes and trees had been removed, while those on top of the wall could shoot an arrow and duck behind the wall. On top of the wall, soldiers had boiling oil and rocks to repel the enemy. Lord, I'm fighting the hardest battle of my life; my wife is non-responsive, so I'm fighting this battle without her help. I'm watching her struggle to breathe. The nurses tell me she is comfortable, but I hear her moaning and her shouts. I've been blessed to be married to the woman I love. My wife has been my lover, my helpmate, and my best friend for fifty-two years; I need strength from you to fight this battle.

"When a soldier outside the walled city was hit with an arrow, he was abandoned on the battle field. However, when a soldier inside the fortress was hit, men who were too old to fight and the ladies were very present giving first-aid. Lord, I'm wounded with the impending death of my wife and it will get worse when she does die. The thought of living my life without her is almost more than I can bear. I will not be able to go on without your help. Thank you, Lord, that you are very present with me.

"For those reasons the psalmist did not fear. Lord, I dread living without my wife, but because you are my refuge, my strength, and you are with me, I don't need to fear the future."

- Discover modern words and examples to express the biblical thoughts

Many Bible texts refer to times and places that differ from our modern day experiences. Rephrase biblical words and phrases to modern expressions which more closely express the meaning the words had when first written. I do not live in a time of walled cities so I tried to come up with modern examples that communicate the thoughts of Psalm 46:1-2.

For example: "Lord, I do not live in a time when I would flee to a walled city for refuge when an enemy was invading. But I do live in "Tornado Alley" where homes have storm shelters, where people seek protection when the weatherman issues a tornado threat. In the same way, you are my storm shelter when I'm threatened with a life-storm. We don't have a walled city that gives us the advantage in the time of war. However, I live in the deep south where it only snows about every five years and drivers are unprepared to drive on the snow. In the same way, when I'm experiencing a storm for which I'm unprepared, you are my four-wheel-drive Jeep with studded snow tires. In the psalmist's day, the soldier who was injured inside the walled city had non-soldiers giving first aid. In the same way, when I have a 911 experience, you are my first responder."

- Use your own words to paraphrase Scripture verses, phrases, or words

Rephrase the Scripture in your own words. The rephrasing may be very close to the text you read and you only substitute a word or two that is easier for you to understand. Use a dictionary, thesaurus, or different Bible translations to come up with different ways to express the biblical thought and then pray it back to God. You may rephrase the whole text or just a word or phrase.

For example: My wife's favorite Scripture was Proverbs 3:5-6, "Trust in the Lord with all your heart and lean not on your own understanding; in all your ways submit to him, and he will make your paths straight" (Pro 3:5-6 NIV). I'm going to focus on the phrase, "lean not on your own understanding."

"God, I'm going to trust you with all my heart, and I'm not going to depend on my way of thinking or my ability to understand. Lord, I trust in you with all my heart because I know my limited understanding could lead me astray. I'm going to trust you with all my heart; I'm not going to depend on my own insight."

- Rephrase the Scripture to make personal application

It was a Sunday when I sat by my wife in a hospice facility. My wife had been non-responsive for over a week. I was waiting for my wife to die. One of my sons sent me a link to 2 Timothy 4:5-6, saying it helped him.

Paul was facing imminent death, and he wrote to Timothy, "But you, keep your head in all situations, endure hardship, do the work of an evangelist, discharge all the duties of your ministry. For I am already being poured out like a drink offering, and the time for my departure is near. I have fought the good fight, I have finished the race, I have kept the faith. Now there is in store for me the crown of righteousness, which the Lord, the righteous Judge, will award to me on that day—and not only to me, but also to all who have longed for his appearing" (2 Tim 4:5-6 NIV).

I rephrased Paul's words to make a personal application. "Lord, my wife of fifty-two years is facing imminent death and will soon leave me. I'm applying Paul's advice to Timothy to myself. Grieving people often make foolish decisions. Help me keep my head in all situations. Help me to endure hardship, especially the hardship of losing my wife and grieving afterwards. Open my eyes to see opportunities to do the work of an evangelist even during my time of grieving. God, you are leaving me behind, so you still have a ministry for me. I will seek to discharge the duties of any ministry you give to me. I'm applying Paul's words about himself to my wife. Doris is being poured out as an offering to you, and the time for her departure is near. She has fought the good fight and is near the finish line of her race. She had a good start in walking with you in faith, and she has kept the faith until the end of her life. Now there is in store for her the crown of righteousness, which the Lord, the righteous Judge, will award to her on that day of her death – and not only to her, but also to all who have longed for Christ's appearing."

9. **Talk to God about Life-lessons Found in Bible Stories**

If we try to apply every verse found in a Bible story as though it applied to our lives, we would have a hard time with verses like the following: "Now go, attack the Amalekites and totally destroy all that belongs to them. Do not spare them; put to death men and women, children and infants, cattle and sheep, camels and donkeys" (1 Sam 15:3 NIV). We need to read Bible stories within their context and apply life-lessons from the story to our lives. God may use the passage in 1 Samuel 15 to speak to us about destroying the worldliness in our lives and leaving no remnant of it. In that instance, we could pray, "Lord, just as you told the Israelites to totally destroy everything that represented the evil of the Amalekites, help me to destroy everything that represents evil in my life."

Talk to God about life-lessons found in the story; do not try to find meaning in every word, phrase, or verse. Don't try to turn every verse into a prayer, because it takes more than one verse to emphasize a life-lesson. Each Bible story gives us so much to pray about. But you have to read the whole story before you can find the life-lessons to pray about. Here is an example.

Bible Story: Jesus Called Matthew (Levi) Luke 5:27-32
Jesus went out and saw a tax collector by the name of Matthew sitting at his tax booth. *(Matthew was also called Levi. Tax*

collectors were Jewish citizens who collaborated with the Roman occupying forces. They were despised and called traitors by fellow Jews.) Jesus invited Matthew the tax collector, "Follow me." Matthew got up, left everything and followed Jesus.

Matthew gave a large banquet for Jesus at his house. A large crowd of tax collectors and others with bad reputations were his guests. The Pharisees and the teachers of the Law of Moses complained to Jesus' disciples, "Why do you eat and drink with tax collectors and sinners?"

Jesus answered them, "Healthy people don't need a doctor. Sick people need a doctor. I didn't come to invite the righteous, but sinners to repentance" (Lk 5:27-32).

Life-lesson:
Jesus invites people to follow Him who are considered by society as bad people. Jesus invited Matthew (Levi) to follow Him (Lk 5:27-32). Matthew had a lucrative, though dishonest, tax collecting business for the occupying Roman government. Fellow Jewish citizens considered him a social outcast who was a traitor to their nation.

Prayer:
"Jesus, I'm aware that the church would not welcome some people whose life-style makes them outcasts. But you came to save such people. Help me to make contact with some of those outcasts and to tell them about Jesus."

Life-lesson:
Sometimes, religious leaders oppose God's work. Religious leaders criticized Jesus for associating with known sinners who were social outcasts (Lk 5:30).

Prayer:
"Lord, I want to be involved in doing your work. When you work in ways that go against my church tradition, I want to cooperate with you and not hinder your work."

CONCLUSION: Praying the Scripture

Bible reading and studying, plus praying, are the primary activities for developing a relationship with God. Other spiritual disciplines such as fasting, meditation, simplicity, worship, confession, are based on the foundation of reading the Bible and praying.

Many think of Bible reading and prayer as separate spiritual activities. First I read the Bible; then I pray. But they can be combined into one practice of "praying scripture."

Scripture that tells us about God the Father, Jesus Christ, and/or the Holy Spirit gives us reasons to praise God. Scripture that tells us what God the Father, Jesus Christ, or the Holy Spirit did, gives us reasons to confess our faith in what they did and express thanksgiving. Scripture that tells us God's commands and what God expects from us, gives us reasons to cry out to God for His help. Scripture that gives us God's promises, gives us reasons to confess our faith. Scripture that shows us how we fail, gives us reasons to confess our sins. Scripture that tells us a story, gives us reasons to tell God the life-lessons we learned from the story and how they apply to our lives.

TIPS TO IMPROVE YOUR PRAYER LIFE

1. **Realize that Believers in Jesus Are Students Who Are Learning to Pray**

   After observing Jesus pray, one of His disciples requested, "Lord, teach us to pray, just as John taught his disciples" (Lk 11:1 NIV).

Commentary:

Christians are students in the school of prayer – learning, developing, getting better, sometimes failing, but always learning.

Application:

We are all students learning to pray. Some are more advanced students than others, but we all need to learn more.

We are students of prayer, but we learn to pray by praying and not by studying prayer. We can't learn to play tennis by just reading a book on tennis. We must get on the tennis court and hit the ball across the net to another player. Books may help us improve our tennis playing, but we'll never learn to play tennis by just reading books. It's the same with prayer. Books may help us pray, but we'll never learn to pray by just reading books. We must pray.

A teacher, prayer coach, a preacher, or a book may give us advice that will help us pray. But we must pray in order to improve our prayer life. I used to play tennis on a weekly basis, and I was teaching one of my sons to play. Together, we took lessons from a tennis coach at a tennis club. The lessons would have done us no good if we had not practiced the tips that the coach taught us. Studies, sermons, and books may give us tips on prayer, but they will only help us if we use them when we spend time praying.

I've played tennis with players who never had a tennis coach, yet they were better players than me. They just started playing and learned by playing. In the same way, many Christians learn to pray by praying. They never studied prayer or read a book on prayer. They learned to pray by praying. Prayer is as easy as breathing for them. They do it without effort.

That effortlessness has not been my experience. I've never been satisfied with my prayer life. I've studied what the Bible teaches about prayer. I've bought and read books on prayer. I have a daily prayer time, but I've always felt a need to improve.

If you are like me and feel a need to improve your prayer life, the following tips may help you. Not all the suggestions will speak to you, but some may.

2. Accept the Fact That Prayer Requires Discipline

We live in a time when people expect instant results. I grew up on a farm, and we raised our own vegetables and meat. I remember mornings when my mother went to the garden early in the morning to pick fresh green beans that had long firm, plump, and crisp pods. Then she brought the beans to the kitchen sink, grabbed a handful and ran them beneath cool, running water, shifting the green beans in her hand as she worked. She used her fingers to gently scrub away any noticeable dirt or debris. Then my mother sat down and worked with each individual bean pod. She'd pinch the stem end of each green bean in between the thumb and index finger of her opposite hand. She'd then quickly yank the stem down toward the body of the bean, snapping it off. Then she would pinch off the curled tip. This was a time-consuming process since she had to trim each bean one-by-one. Then my mother cooked the beans. However, my daughters-in-law go to the grocery store and buy beans in a can or frozen package that are ready to cook. They then return home and instantly start cooking the beans.

Neither of my daughters-in-law would accept a gift basket of fresh green beans. They want beans that are ready to cook.

Accept the fact that there is no quick easy way to improve your prayer life. If people are to grow in their prayer life, they must daily separate a time for prayer, and spend time praying. Sometimes prayer is hard work, and sometimes it is hard to pray. When it is hard to pray, we need to work hard at praying. Prayer requires discipline.

3. Schedule a Specific Time for Bible Reading and Prayer

If possible, pray at the same time each day. Schedule a time for prayer. It is possible to pray anytime, anywhere, and under any condition. However, most people will not take time to pray unless they schedule some part of each day for prayer.

4. **Choose a Place for Prayer**

Try to find a place that is quiet and free from interruption. It is best to have a designated place for prayer rather than hunt for a different spot each day. Choose a specific place to pray away from distractions so you can concentrate. Ringing phones, pinging ipads, and children arguing over a toy will sabotage your prayer time.

5. **Choose a Posture for Praying That Is the Most Comfortable and the Least Distracting**

A person can pray in any position: sitting, kneeling, lying prostrate on the floor, and standing with hands and head lifted toward the heavens.

Find a position that is the most comfortable and the least distracting.

Sometimes I kneel, sometimes I stand and raise my hands above my head, and sometimes I lie prostrate on the floor. But most of the time I sit up straight in a chair when I'm praying.

6. **Pray Aloud**

Many people can pray silently with their mouth closed and thinking prayers in their minds. But for many of us, the silent prayer is a quick ticket to dreamland. Praying out loud forces us to concentrate on what we are praying about and forces us to form intelligent sentences.

7. **Make a Prayer List or Keep a Prayer Journal to Keep Track of Your Prayer Needs**

This can be done several ways. Prayer needs can be listed by category like "Church," "Family," "People with needs," or "Unsaved friends." Or they may be listed by the days of the week. Each day you pray for a different set of needs. You may want to include prayers for each day for a different area of society that has an influence on our lives. Seven categories could include: 1) church and religion; 2) family and home; 3) media; 4) government; 5) education; 6) business and commerce; 7) arts and entertainment.

Years ago, I was greeting people after preaching and a lady asked me to pray for her surgery. I failed to write down her prayer request. About six weeks later, the woman saw me and told me, "God answered our prayers and my surgery was a success." I didn't have the courage to say, "God answered <u>your</u> prayers. I forgot to pray for you."

For me, prayer requests not written down become forgotten prayer requests.

I used to keep my prayer requests in a notebook. Now I keep them in a file on my computer. I use the following format:

DATE	REQUEST	ANSWER

This format helps me keep track of what I'm praying for and when I began praying for it. I leave a space to jot down the answer when it comes. This helps me to be aware of God's answer so I can thank Him promptly. Sometimes answers to prayer come in the back door and I don't want them to slip by me. Recording my prayer requests and then recording how God answered them has increased my confidence in prayer.

The prayer journal is another variation. In the prayer journal you write a personal prayer to the Lord on a daily basis.

8. **Learn to Pray Quick Prayers**

If the thought of laboring over a topic wears you out, pray short, sincere prayers instead.

When I was a young man in 1970, I could send up to a fifteen word telegraph for $2.25. After fifteen words, I paid ten cents per word. Today's youth use "Twitter." Twitter is an online news and social networking service where users post and interact with messages. "Tweets" are restricted to 140 characters. Condense your prayers to a few words for "Telegraph" or "Twitter-length prayers."

9. **Learn from Those Whose Prayer Life Is More Advanced than Yours**

We are all students who are learning to pray. Some are more advanced than others. So pray with and learn from those who are more advanced than you in their prayer life. When I played tennis,

I discovered that the best way to improve my game was to play with players who were better than me. Praying with people who are more advanced in their prayer life helps me grow in prayer.

Often the best teachers are those who are just a little more advanced than we are. My wife was a patient in the hospital, and she was receiving an IV. A second semester nursing student was assisting the nurse. The student nurse tried to determine how many milliliters of medicine were still in an IV sack. The second semester student asked a third semester student to help her. The third semester nursing student bubbled with enthusiasm as she explained things to the second semester student. However, the RN showed little enthusiasm when she explained things to the student nurse. Often, those who recently gained new understanding about prayer are the ones most excited about helping others.

SCRIPTURAL PRECONDITIONS FOR BELIEVERS TO RECEIVE ANSWERS TO THEIR PRAYERS

1. **Remain in Jesus**
Jesus promised His disciples that if they remained in Him, their prayers would be answered. "If you remain in me...ask whatever you wish, and it will be done for you" (Jn 15:7 NIV). To remain in Jesus means to depend on one's connection to Jesus in the same way as grape branches depend on their connection to the grapevine that grows from the ground.

2. **Christ's Words Remain in You**
Jesus promised His disciples that if His words remained in them, their prayers would be answered. "If...my words remain in you, ask whatever you wish, and it will be done for you." (Jn 15:7 NIV).
For Christ's words to remain in you, you must have a conscious acceptance of the authority of His word, and make a conscious decision to keep reading or hearing His words and thinking about them. The results will be that Christ's words influence your thoughts, attitudes, speech and actions.

3. **Ask in the Name of Jesus**
In the context of listening to His disciples' questions about His resurrection, Jesus promised them that after the resurrection they would no longer question him; they would present their petitions to the Father in His name and the Father would respond to their needs. Jesus promised, "In that day you will no longer ask me anything. Very truly I tell you, my Father will give you whatever you ask in my name. Until now you have not asked for anything in my name. Ask and you will receive, and your joy will be complete" (Jn 16:23-24 NIV).
The believer prays with the attitude that he is going to heaven's bank with a check signed by Jesus, knowing he himself has no funds deposited there.

Believers can present their own petitions to God the Father in Jesus' name. "In that day you will ask in my name. I am not saying that I will ask the Father on your behalf. No, the Father himself loves you because you have loved me and have believed that I came from God" (Jn 16:26-27 NIV). Believers standing with God depends on the merits of Jesus. Because of His work and their relationship to Him by faith, they can approach the Father directly with their petitions.

4. **Obey God's Commands**
The Apostle John said that believers have confidence before God and receive from Him anything they ask, because they obey His commands and do what pleases Him. "Dear friends, if our hearts do not condemn us, we have confidence before God and receive from him anything we ask, because we keep his commands ..." (1 Jn 3:21-22 NIV). Do what God asks, and God will hear your prayer and respond as He sees best.

5. **Do What Is Pleasing to God**
The Apostle John said that believers have confidence before God and receive from Him anything they ask, because they obey His commands and do what pleases Him (Jn 3:21-22). The believer goes beyond obeying biblical commands; he tries to please God in everything. There are subjects on which the Bible is silent; however, the believer who seeks to please God in relation to those subjects will have answers to his prayers.

6. **Pray According to God's Will**
- The motive of the prayer request should be according to God's will.

The Apostle James said that believers pray, yet don't receive because they ask with the wrong motive. "When you ask, you do not receive, because you ask with wrong motives, that you may spend what you get on your pleasure" (Jam 4:3 NIV).

A person can request something that is according to God's will but with a motive that is contrary to it. For example: a person can desire to teach the Bible so he can be recognized by others as a church leader.

- **Discover God's Will in the Bible**
The Bible teaches us many things about God's will.

- It is God's will that believers obey biblical commands.

The Apostle John said that believers have confidence before God and receive from Him anything they ask, because they obey His commands and do what pleases Him (1 Jn 3:21-22).

- It is God's will that people believe His promises.

God considered Abraham righteous because Abraham believed His promises (Gen 15:6). An example of one of God's promises is: If a person facing trials lacks wisdom, he should ask God, believing God will give him the needed wisdom, and it will be given him (Jam 1:5).

- **Discover God's Will by Following the Guidance of the Holy Spirit**
    - Jesus promised that the Holy Spirit is a Counselor who will teach His followers.

"But the Advocate, the Holy Spirit, whom the Father will send in my name, will teach you all things and will remind you of everything I have said to you" (Jn 14:26 NIV).

The Holy Spirit guides the follower of Jesus to the truth. "But when he, the Spirit of truth, comes, he will guide you into all the truth" (Jn 16:13 NIV).

- The Holy Spirit helps believers pray.

"In the same way, the Spirit helps us in our weakness. We do not know what we ought to pray for, but the Spirit himself intercedes for us through wordless groans. And he who searches our hearts knows the mind of the Spirit, because the Spirit intercedes for God's people in accordance with the will of God" (Rom 8:26-27 NIV).

- The Holy Spirit leads believers

"For those who are led by the Spirit of God are the children of God" (Rom 8:14 NIV).

The Greek word translated "led" was often used to depict animals that were led by a rope tied around their necks. Paul used this word to tell us that we should let the Holy Spirit lead us in every part of our lives. We should be so surrendered to God that wherever the Holy Spirit tells us to go or whatever He tells us to do, we should simply be obedient and follow.

I've had dogs that resisted being led and they pulled against the leash so they could go where they wanted to go. When a dog refused to follow my leading, I yanked the leash and forced him to follow me. The Holy Spirit wants to lead us; however, our sinful human nature doesn't like to be led. But the Holy Spirit does not force us to follow Him. The human will and the sinful nature are strong, and they don't want to surrender control to someone else — and that includes being led by the Holy Spirit. The choice is ours if we follow the Holy Spirit's leading

How do we recognize the Spirit's guidance? How do we discern between our own desires and His leading? The Holy Spirit does not speak with audible words. He guides us through our own consciences and other quiet, subtle ways. The most important way to recognize the Holy Spirit's guidance is to know God's word. Scripture is the ultimate source of wisdom about how we should live; believers should search the Bible and meditate on Bible verses. When reading Scripture, the Holy Spirit speaks to us and reveals God's will for our lives. When we know the Bible, the Holy Spirit reminds us of specific scriptures when we need them most. God's word helps us to discern whether or not our desires come from the Holy Spirit or from our desires or sinful nature. We must test our inclinations against Scripture – the Holy Spirit will never urge us to do anything contrary to God's word. He will never lead us into sin.

It is also necessary for us to be in continual prayer with the Father. Prayer time is a time to both converse with God and to listen to God. We talk to God and the Holy Spirit talks to us.

We have the choice whether or not to accept the Holy Spirit's guidance. When we know the will of God but do not follow it, we are resisting the Spirit's work in our lives. Our desire to follow our own way grieves Him. When we know the will of God and follow it, we will know how to pray according to the will of God.

7. **Believe**

There is a strong connection in believing that God will answer our prayer and receiving the answer to our prayer. "'Have faith in God,' Jesus answered. 'Truly I tell you, if anyone says to this mountain, Go, throw yourself into the sea, and does not doubt in their heart but believes that what they say will happen, it will be done for them. Therefore I tell you, whatever you ask for in prayer, believe that you have received it, and it will be yours'" (Mk 11:22-24 NIV).

The doubting or double-minded person will not receive anything form the Lord when he prays. "But when you ask, you must believe and not doubt, because the one who doubts is like a wave of the sea, blown and tossed by the wind. That person should not expect to receive anything from the Lord. Such a person is double-minded and unstable in all they do" (Jam 1:7-8). It is as though the double-minded person has two minds when he prays. One mind declares "I believe," while the other declares, "I don't believe."

The Christian has reason to believe that God does what He promises! However, unless there is a Biblical promise, or there is clear illumination from the Holy Spirit, there is no reason to have faith. The Christian has no reason to expect God to do what He does not promise to do. The Holy Spirit will never give a promise that contradicts the Scriptures.

8. **Continue to Pray Without Becoming Discouraged**

Jesus told a parable about a man who received a traveler into his home late at night, and he had no food for the traveler. The man went to his neighbor's house to borrow bread. The neighbor didn't want to get out of bed, but because the man kept insisting, the neighbor finally got up and gave him what he needed. The reluctant sleepy neighbor in Christ's story yielded to insistent begging (Lk 11:5-8).

After telling the parable of the man begging his neighbor for bread at midnight, Jesus encouraged His disciples to be intense and insistent in prayer by asking, seeking, and knocking (Lk 11:9-10).

The words, "ask, seek, and knock," in a different context, are also found in Matthew 7:7-8, but the purpose is the same in both passages, that people should not cease to pray, and that they should pray with greater and greater urgency.

There are three levels of prayer: ask, seek, and knock. To seek is more than to ask, and to knock is more than to seek.

Jesus promised that those who ask and keep on asking, who seek and keep on seeking, and who knock and keep on knocking will experience results. This emphasized that those who are intense and insistent in prayer will be heard by God.

Jesus told His disciples the parable of the Unjust Judge to show them that they should always pray and not give up (Lk 18:1-8).

The praying person should continue to take his request to God in prayer until God answers the prayer or the person becomes convinced that his request is not according to God's will.

9. **Pray with a Heavy Heart**
When experiencing a crisis, prayer becomes a time of desperate pleading with a heavy heart. Some pastors were at a camp for a spiritual retreat, and they were discussing the best position for praying. One argued for kneeling, another for lying prostrate on the floor, and another for standing with hands raised upward.

An employee of the campgrounds overheard the discussion and told the pastors, "The best prayer I've ever prayed was when my feet were up and my head was down."

One pastor said, "I've never seen that position mentioned in the Bible; I don't know anyone who prays in that position."

The camp employee said, "I fell into a well with my head facing down and my feet facing upward. In that position, I prayed like I've never prayed before."

The person who is desperate prays with a heavy heart.

Examples of people who prayed with a heavy heart:
- Abraham.

On one occasion, the Lord spoke to Abram (before his name was changed to Abraham) in a vision, "Abram. Your reward will be great."

Abram prayed, "O Sovereign Lord, what good are your blessings when I have no son?" (Gen 15:1-21).

On another occasion, the Lord told Abraham, that He was going to visit Sodom and Gomorrah. Abraham pleaded with God not to kill the good people along with the wicked (Gen 18:16-33).

- Jacob.

Jacob had cheated his brother Esau out of the blessing his father had promised him. Esau wanted to kill Jacob, so Jacob fled from Esau. Years later, Jacob was returning home and he was informed that Esau was coming to meet him with 400 armed men. Jacob spent the night wrestling with God (Gen 32:22-31).

- Jeremiah.

After God allowed the Babylonians to destroy Jerusalem, Jeremiah described his condition while praying, "My eyes fail from weeping, I am in torment within; my heart is poured out on the ground because my people are destroyed, because children and infants faint in the streets of the city" (Lam 2:11 NIV).

- Jesus, in the Garden of Gethsemane.

In the Garden of Gethsemane, Jesus felt an agonizing distress, and fell face-down to the ground and prayed, "Father, everything is possible for you. Take this cup of suffering from me. Yet let your will be done rather than mine" (Mat 26:36-39; Mk 14:32-36). Jesus was in such anguish, and He prayed so earnestly that His sweat was like drops of blood falling to the ground (Lk 22:44).

The person who is experiencing a crisis should react by desperately pleading with God with a heavy heart.

10. **Be United When Praying Together**

Jesus told His disciples, "Again, truly I tell you that if two of you on earth agree about anything they ask for, it will be done for them by my Father in heaven" (Mat 18:19 NIV).

Matthew 18:15-20 gives instructions for dealing with a believer in Christ who has sinned against another believer. Matthew 18:19 is part of Christ's instructions to a local church as to how to confront an erring member. Verse 19 does not constitute a prayer promise to individual Christians.

Conflict between believers who pray together impedes the answers of their prayers. Jesus only demands an agreement among two people, but Jesus' desire is that this Christian agreement is extended to include all believers of the world. Jesus prayed to His Father for the believers in him, "...That all of them may be one, Father, just as you are in me and I am in you" (Jn 17:21 NIV).

BIBLICAL EXPLANATIONS OF WHAT IMPEDES GOD FROM ANSWERING PRAYER

Some things impede God from answering prayers besides not reaching the "Pre-conditions to Receive Answer to the Prayer" of the item listed.

1. **Praying with Wrong Motives**
"When you ask, you do not receive, because you ask with wrong motives, that you may spend what you get on your pleasures" (Ja 4:3 NIV).

The praying believer creates a barrier that interferes with God answering his prayer when the motive of his request is self-indulgence or self-promotion.

The pastor who prays for more converts to Christ, so he can be recognized as baptizing more than other pastors is praying for a good thing with wrong motives.

2. **Lack of Thankfulness**
On one occasion, Jesus met ten men who had leprosy. Jesus told the ten men, "Go, show yourselves to the priests." The men left and on the way to the priests, they were cleansed. Only one of them returned to Jesus, praising God in a loud voice.

Jesus asked, "Ten men were healed! Where are the other nine?" (Lk 17:11-19).

It is more rare to find gratitude than faith.

The Bible commands us to give thanks to God.

"Do not be anxious about anything, but in every situation, by prayer and petition, with thanksgiving, present your requests to God" (Phip 4:6 NIV).

"Give thanks in all circumstances; for this is God's will for you in Christ Jesus" (1 Thess 5:18 NIV).

Lack of gratitude for God's blessings and answered prayers may hinder God from answering new requests.

3. **Unconfessed and Unabandoned Sins**

Unconfessed and unabandoned sins interfere with God answering our prayers.

The psalmist testified, "If I had cherished sin in my heart, the Lord would not have listened" (Psa 66:18).

"Surely the arm of the Lord is not too short to save, nor his ear too dull to hear. But your iniquities have separated you from your God; your sins have hidden his face from you, so that he will not hear" (Is 59:1-2 NIV).

Jesus healed a man blind from birth. The former blind man testified, "We know that God does not listen to sinners. He listens to the godly person who does his will" (Jn 9:31 NIV).

Unconfessed and unabandoned sins can impede God's answering our prayers. The sin that impedes the answer of the prayer can be one that the believer doesn't consider a sin. Unanswered prayer should cause the believer to examine himself to see if he has unconfessed and unabandoned sins. Unanswered prayers should lead to our praying the prayer of the psalmist, "Search me, God, and know my heart; test me and know my anxious thoughts. See if there is any offensive way in me, and lead me in the way everlasting" (Psa 139:23-24 NIV).

Not all unanswered prayer is caused by sin; however, anytime someone has unanswered prayer, he should do a self-examination to determine if he has unconfessed sins.

4. **Idols in the Heart**

God asked if He should even allow the person who has idols in his heart to pray, "Son of man, these men have set up idols in their hearts and put wicked stumbling blocks before their faces. Should I let them inquire of me at all?" (Eze 14:3 NIV).

Some Israelite elders came to Ezekiel (Eze 14:1-8). The Bible doesn't tell us why they came to Ezekiel because God cut them off before they made their request. God told Ezekiel that He would not hear their requests because they had set up idols in their hearts. The Bible neither tells us what their request to God would have been, nor what their particular idols were (Eze 14:3).

Idols in the heart are not those on a pedestal or in a shrine. They are those that are in the mind and heart. Anything we put before God is an idol. Anything can become our idol: family, career, political position, a vice, lust, music, sports, hobbies, video games or other entertainment, pride, self-promotion, the pursuit of money, the pursuit of a position or the pursuit of happiness.

Some Christian counselors emphasize four "core idols" that dominate our hearts: power, control, approval, and comfort.
- Power. If the core idol in our heart is power, we'll become domineering, harsh, and abusive.
- Control. If the core idol in our heart is control, we'll worry all the time; we'll often lose our temper; or we'll manipulate others to get our way.
- Approval. If the core idol in our heart is approval, our life will be plagued by self-pity, envy, hurt feelings, and inadequacy.
- Comfort. If the core idol in our heart is comfort, we won't be able to say "no" to the pleasures of food or sex or drugs or pornography.

None of the four core idols is evil on its own. It's when they become the ultimate goal in our lives — commanding our obedience and ruling our emotions — that they become an idol in the heart and displace God as our Master. An idol in the heart may not be something bad; it may be desiring something good, yet in excess.

Questions that will help you determine the idols in your heart:
- What makes you angry — uncontrollably, vehemently angry?
- What causes you to fear — panicked, terror-stricken, paralyzing fear?
- What drives you to sadness — despairing, inconsolable sadness?

What in your life, if threatened or lost, drives you over the emotional edge of anger, fear, or sadness? That is the idol in your heart. Idols in our hearts prevent God from hearing and answering our prayers.

5. **Lack of Compassion for the Needy**
"Whoever shuts their ears to the cry of the poor will also cry out and not be answered" (Pro 21:13 NIV).

Jesus told His disciples, "Give, and it will be given to you. A good measure, pressed down, shaken together and running over, will be poured into your lap. For with the measure you use, it will be measured to you" (Lk 6:38 NIV).

The person who ignores and lacks compassion for the needy will experience his prayers being ignored by God. The person who wants to receive from God needs to help the needy.

6. **Refusing to Forgive Others**
In the Sermon on the Mount Jesus said, "For if you forgive other people when they sin against you, your heavenly Father will also forgive you. But if you do not forgive others their sins, your Father will not forgive your sins" (Mat 6:14-15 NIV).

God answers the person's prayers whose sins are forgiven. The person who doesn't forgive other people is in sin, is not forgiven by God, and doesn't receive from God answers to his prayers.

7. **Disrespecting One's Marriage Partner**
"Husbands, in the same way be considerate as you live with your wives, and treat them with respect as the weaker partner and as heirs with you of the gracious gift of life, so that nothing will hinder your prayers" (1 Pet 3:7 NIV).

The person who mistreats his spouse hinders God from answering his prayers.

8. **Pride**
Jesus told the parable to some who were sure that they were upright but despised everyone else, "Two men went up to the temple to pray. One was a Pharisee and the other was a tax collector. The Pharisee stood in front of everyone and prayed about himself, `God, I thank you that I'm not like other people. I'm not a robber. I'm not an evildoer. I haven't committed adultery. I'm definitely not like this tax collector. I fast twice a week and tithe on all my income.'

"However, the tax collector stood a distance from the people. He wouldn't even look up to heaven. Instead he beat his breast and said, `God, have mercy on me, a sinner.'

"I tell you that the tax collector, rather than the Pharisee, went home justified, being approved by God. For everyone who honors himself will be humbled, and he who humbles himself will be honored" (Lk 18:9-14).

The person who prays in the spirit of congratulating himself is deceiving himself with his arrogant prayer. God does not hear the prayer of the prideful person.

9. **Satan and/or Satanic Forces Can Delay Answers to Prayer**
Satan impeded Daniel from receiving the answer to his prayer for twenty-one days (Dan 10:1-13).

Paul advised the Ephesians, "Finally, be strong in the Lord and in his mighty power. Put on the full armor of God, so that you can take your stand against the devil's schemes. For our struggle is not against flesh and blood, but against the rulers, against the authorities, against the powers of this dark world and against the spiritual forces of evil in the heavenly realms" (Eph 6:10-12 NIV).

Often, Christians on earth are unaware of the spiritual war where satanic forces battle against God and his angels. Job was unaware that Satan was assaulting him as part of a spiritual war against God (Job chapters 1 - 2).

Satanic forces battling against God's forces can sometimes delay God's answering our prayers.

10. **God May Use Unanswered Prayer to Build Character**
Paul wrote, "Not only so, but we also glory in our sufferings, because we know that suffering produces perseverance; perseverance, character; and character, hope. And hope does not put us to shame, because God's love has been poured out into our hearts through the Holy Spirit, who has been given to us" (Rom 5:3-5 NIV).

James the brother of Jesus wrote, "Consider it pure joy, my brothers and sisters, whenever you face trials of many kinds, because you know that the testing of your faith produces perseverance. Let perseverance finish its work so that you may be mature and complete, not lacking anything" (Jam 1:2-4 NIV).

We believers are concerned about our comfort; God is concerned about our character. If it takes problems and trials to give us character, God lets the problems come. When we pray for comfort, freedom from pain and difficulty, and a life of luxury and ease; God may send us problems, pain, sorrow, stress, and upheaval to build up our character. We hate the process that makes us spiritually mature and more like Christ because it involves problems, pain, sorrow, stress, and upheaval. However, we want the end product: spiritual maturity. So God may use unanswered prayer as a means to build up our character and give us spiritual maturity.

After my father died, when I was fourteen years old, an uncle by marriage cheated my mother out of money for timber sold from our farm. That money would have paid for my university education. It was not God's will for my uncle to steal from us. But God did use his theft to help me. I became a barber to work my way through the university. In the barber shop, I learned more about how to deal with all kinds of people than in my university or seminary.

REASONS NOT FOUND IN THE BIBLE WHY GOD MAY APPEAR NOT TO ANSWER PRAYERS

God hears our prayers, but He may answer them with a "No," or a "Yes," or a "Later," or an "I've got something better for you." God's "No" is not rejection, but redirection. "Wait" is an answer. Delay is not denial.

God knows exactly what He's doing when He says "no" to our prayers, when He seems to put us on hold, or when it appears that He isn't listening at all.

1. **God May Be Waiting to Give Us Something Better Than We Requested**

"'For I know the plans I have for you,' declares the Lord, 'plans to prosper you and not to harm you, plans to give you hope and a future'" (Jer 29:11 NIV).

"'For my thoughts are not your thoughts, neither are your ways my ways,' declares the Lord. 'As the heavens are higher than the earth, so are my ways higher than your ways and my thoughts than your thoughts'" (Is 55:8-9 NIV).

Unanswered prayer can be a greater gift than getting what we requested in prayer. Scripture reminds us that God's ways are not always our ways. Two things I know: (1) God is real and (2) I am not God. Therefore, God knows what is best for me, and I may be mistaken when I petition God for something that I think I need. God's "unanswered" prayer may be the best answer for me.

Garth Brooks sang a country song, "Unanswered Prayer." A man runs into his high school sweetheart at a football game. He reminisces how he once prayed that this girl would be his wife. Then he thanks God for not answering his original prayer because God gave him a better woman. He sees his wife as one of the blessings in his life. The chorus advises the listener that, if God is not answering his or her prayers, that "just because He doesn't answer doesn't mean He don't care," and that unanswered prayers are "some of God's greatest gifts."

A story is told about a man who played golf, who helped a king. The king asked the golf player to demand anything he wanted as a gift for the service he had rendered. The golfer asked for a golf club. He was anxious to receive his golf club and went to the mail day after day to check if it had arrived. Days turned to months but in the end the king gave him a large piece of land that had a new club house and golf course.

Sometimes, God doesn't answer our prayer as requested because He plans to give us something better than we requested.

2. **God May Not Answer Our Prayers Because They Are Vague Generalities**
If we ask God to "bless everyone in our church," or "forgive everyone in town," it would be impossible to see the prayer answered in any concrete way. Vague general prayers have no specific and concrete application.

3. **It May Be That the Time Is Not Right for God to Answer Your Prayer**
The Gospel of Luke begins with the story of priest Zechariah. Priest Zechariah was married to Elizabeth. Both Zechariah and Elizabeth were good people who pleased the Lord God. They had no children because Elizabeth couldn't conceive. Both of them were very old. One day Zechariah's division of priests was on duty and he was serving as a priest. Zechariah entered the Lord's temple to burn incense. Suddenly, the angel Gabriel appeared. Zechariah was terrified. The angel calmed him, "Don't be afraid, Zechariah; God has heard your prayer. Your wife Elizabeth will bear you a son." Zechariah completed his time of priestly service and returned home. His wife Elizabeth became pregnant (Lk 1:5-25).

As a newly married young man with a young wife, Zechariah began to pray that God would give them a child. God heard his prayer; however, God did not answer it until Zechariah and Elizabeth were very old. God waited until He considered the time was right to answer Zechariah's prayer.

God may have looked at our life and judged that the time is not right for us to receive that blessing when we asked. God is a God of process, and sometimes we must wait on the process and mature before He lets us have certain things. Often, God does not give us what He promises all at once. For instance, God anointed young David king but kept David from the throne until the right time; after Saul and Jonathan's deaths.

4. **God Gives People Freedom of Choice; Therefore, Prayer Can Not Be Used to Force Others to Do as One Requests**
God gives people the right to make choices; that means God won't force people to change in answer to our prayer.

The wife can not use prayer to force her husband to be faithful to her. The unemployed can't use prayer to force an employer to give him a job. Parents can't use prayer to force a child to stop using drugs.

5. **Unanswered Prayer Can Improve a Person's Relationship with God**
By not giving us what we want, as soon as we ask for it, God is ensuring that we will keep coming back to ask. He doesn't want the role of a Santa Claus in our life. He wants a relationship. God will do whatever it takes, either in blessing or withholding blessing, in order to keep us clinging to Him.

6. **The Reason for Unanswered Prayer May Remain a Mystery**
Job never understood the reasons for his suffering. He didn't know about Satan's trying to prove a point to God by attacking him.

I could easily start a file with questions that I do not have the answers to or unanswered prayers that I don't understand.

As I wrote this, I did not understand why God allowed my wife's health to decline. I didn't understand why she died the week of Christmas. And yet, at the same time, God blessed me with excellent health and enabled me to continue to be a long distance runner.

7. **God May Want to Teach Us Lessons by His Apparent "Withholding"**
As I look back through the rearview mirror of my life, I'm aware that the times I grew most in my relationship with God and when I learned the most valuable life-lessons were during difficult times. More serious thinking takes place in a hospital room than in any university classroom. God taught me more during the times when

I was suffering than during the times when everything seemed to be going well.

I hated the suffering my wife experienced during her declining health and lingering process of death. Yet, I'm aware that God taught me many biblical and life-lessons through the process. My frustration with my prayers being unanswered led me to write this book.

God's apparent "withholding" and "denials" may be the means He uses to teach us lessons He wants us to learn.

8. Unanswered Prayers Can Enable Believers to Minister to Others

"Praise be to the God and Father of our Lord Jesus Christ, the Father of compassion and the God of all comfort, who comforts us in all our troubles, so that we can comfort those in any trouble with the comfort we ourselves receive from God." (2 Cor 1:4 NIV).

When our oldest son was eleven years old, he developed a low grade fever that remained with him for six weeks. The doctor warned us that he did not know if our son would live or die. The person who most helped me was a pastor whose two year old daughter had recovered from open-heart surgery. My son and daughter-in-law have experienced their seven year old daughter having stage four cancer for six years. They have become like magnets who attract other parents whose children are suffering from chronic illness.

One of my best friends died the year before my wife died. The week my wife died, my friend's widow advised me, "Look for others who have lost a spouse because they will know what you are going through. They are the safe ones to talk to."

9. God Plans to Use What Is Undesirable to Us for the Good of Others and to Advance His Kingdom

Jesus was walking down a street in Jerusalem and saw a man who had been blind since birth. His disciples asked, "Teacher, whose sin caused this man to be born blind? Was it his own sin or was it his parents' sin?"

Jesus replied, "Neither his sins nor his parents sins caused his blindness. This happened so that the work of God might be seen in his life."

Jesus spit on the ground, made mud with his spit, smeared mud on the man's eyes and commanded, "Go, wash off the mud in the Pool of Siloam." The blind man went, washed off the mud, and came back seeing (Jn 9:1-12).

Just as the man suffering from blindness enabled the work of God to be seen in his life, the undesirable things that happen to us when our prayers are unanswered may enable the work of God to be seen in our lives.

10. **Sometimes Christians Pray at Cross Purposes with Other Believers. God Has to Say "No" to One in Order to Say "Yes" to the Other**

Two coaches attend the same church. One coaches the Bulldogs, the other coaches the Wildcats. The Bulldogs and the Wildcats are playing on Friday, and each coach is praying for his team to win.

Two Christians are applying for the same job and each is praying, telling God he needs the job in order to feed his family.

Mrs. Jones is praying for a sunny day for her daughter's outdoor wedding, and Mr. Farmer is praying for rain because if the drought continues, it will kill his crops.

11. **God's "No" May Be for Our Protection**

Sometimes God knows that to say "yes" to our prayers would bring us unforeseen harm. An earthly father who has many faults will not give his son a stone when his son asks for bread. Neither will our heavenly Father give us something useless when we ask for something we need. Also, an earthly father who has many faults will not give his son a snake when his son asked for a fish. Neither will our heavenly Father give us something harmful when we ask for something useful (Mat 7:9-11).

If a child mistakenly asks for something useless, the earthly father would not honor his request. If a child goes fishing with his father and sees a rock on the river bank that looks just like bread, and he asks his father to give him the rock to eat, the father will give him bread instead of the rock he requests. In the same way, if we ask our heavenly Father for something that is useless for us, He will give us something useful. In the same manner, the child may see something moving in the fishing net and thinks it is a fish, but it is a snake. If the child asks his father to give him the snake, that he mistakenly thinks is a fish, the father would refuse his request. If we ask our heavenly Father for something that He knows will harm us, He will deny our prayer request.

A business man told about finishing a business meeting earlier than expected. He took a taxi to the airport and prayed during the ride that he would be able to catch an earlier flight home; however, the plane was full, and he wasn't able to catch the plane. The man was disappointed that his prayer was not answered until later in the day when he heard on the news that the plane had crashed.

12. What We Perceive as Unanswered Prayers May Be God's Perfect Answers

A better term for "Unanswered Prayer" could be "Unexpected Answers." We may be calling something an unanswered prayer, when we may need to understand the unanswered prayer is God's perfect answer for us. It may take us years to realize the blessings of unanswered prayer; in fact, we may not understand this until eternity. God our Father loves us too much to give us everything we ask for. I have lived long enough to thank God that many of my prayers were not answered as I requested. Many times, if God had granted our prayer request, it would have been a mistake for us and a mistake for others. In our shortsightedness, we ask for things that could harm us. When I was in the university, I prayed for a specific English major to become my wife. It didn't happen. Five years later, God gave me a marvelous woman who became my wife for fifty-two years.

13. God May Be Using Unanswered Prayer for Our Spiritual Benefit

It may be that God does not give us what we asked for because God is using our unanswered prayers for our spiritual benefit. The Lord may be using unanswered prayer to grow a deeper reliance and trust in Him. The Canaanite woman cried out desperately to our Lord for mercy and healing for her daughter when He visited the region of Tyre and Sidon (Mat 15:21-28). She was a non-Jew and she was a woman; two reasons the Jews ignored her. Jesus didn't seem to answer her petitions, but He knew all about her situation and granted her request.

PRAYER NOT ANSWERED AS REQUESTED

Many mysteries will only be revealed when we cross into eternity. I don't understand why my father died of a heart attack when I was fourteen years old. I don't understand why God allowed an uncle to steal money from my newly widowed mother. I don't understand why my wife miscarried the baby we dreamed to hold in our arms. I don't understand why a church plant failed because we lost our Sunday rent at a school and could not find another place to rent for Sunday meetings. I don't understand why some of the sick I prayed for were healed while others died. I don't understand why one of my granddaughters had stage four cancer for six years. When I began writing this book on prayer, I didn't understand why my wife had declining health. I didn't understand why she needed to go into assisted living. I didn't understand why she needed to go into hospice care. I didn't understand why her funeral would be five days before Christmas. I have many questions stemming from what I perceive as unanswered prayers.

The incident that provoked me to write this book occurred at a church. The church had been praying for a church member's son who had cancer. Doctors recommended a treatment and informed the family that they were not sure he would survive the treatment, but they were certain he would die without the treatment. One Sunday, the father informed the church that their prayers had been answered, and his son was responding to treatment. Church members shouted, "Thank you, Jesus," "Praise the Lord," "That is the kind of God we serve," and "Our God answers prayer."

I rejoiced in hearing the father's God-story; however, I felt frustrated. I went to church by myself because my wife was home with complications from cirrhosis of the liver. Also, my six year old granddaughter had suffered from stage four cancer for five years, and her cancer had not responded to any treatment. We had prayed that our granddaughter would be accepted into an experimental treatment. The previous week, the doctors informed our son and his wife that our granddaughter was not a candidate for experimental treatment. The church did not hear my God-stories of how God was our Ebenezer, the Lord who has been with my wife and me until now. I didn't share how the certainty that God was with us helped us face her declining health and make the decision to leave the house we loved and move into assisted living. Neither did I share how God has helped our family deal with our granddaughter's cancer. If I had shared my God-stories, there would have been no shouts of joy.

On another Sunday, parents shared their God-story about how God had answered their prayer for their son who was addicted to drugs. He had just checked into a Christian rehab center. However, another family did not share how their prayers were unanswered and their family member had overdosed on drugs and died. That family did not share any God-stories of struggling to deal with a family member's addiction to pain medicine and how God was helping them deal with her death. If they had shared their God-story, there would have been no shouts of joy.

It seemed to me that our church saw winners and losers in the game of prayer. The father whose prayers were answered was a winner. And I, whose prayers were unanswered, was a loser. It was like March Madness Basketball. Winners jump and shout for joy on the way to the locker room, while losers bow their heads and silently walk to the locker room. Church members with answered prayers joyfully share their God-stories, while people with unanswered prayers suffer in silence. The church treats prayers the way doctors treat difficult surgeries. Doctors gather on the front steps of the hospital before TV cameras to joyfully report successful surgeries; however, they slip the corpse of failed surgeries out the back door.

While my wife's health was declining, a pastor visited and prayed with us several times. But his visits and prayers did more harm than help. The pastor teaches the ABC's of prayer: "Ask, believe, and claim." <u>Ask</u> God for what you want. <u>Believe</u> that God has already answered your prayer. <u>Claim</u> that God is in the process of answering you. Before your prayer petitions have been answered, publicly claim the answered prayer by publicly giving thanks to God for His answer. The pastor teaches that if you follow the ABC's of prayer, you become pregnant with the answer of your prayer. Wait and God will give birth to your prayer. The pastor does not consider the possibility that God's answer to a prayer request could be a "No." Even mentioning that possibility is seen by him as evidence of unbelief. When the pastor talked that way, I felt that he was accusing me of being responsible for my wife's cirrhosis and approaching death. He was placing the blame on me because I didn't rightly use the ABC's of prayer.

My wife's suffering intensified. I prayed for wisdom to know how long I should allow medical science to fight for her life, and when it would become cruel to allow procedures and medicine to prolong her suffering. I was praying for wisdom, yet the pastor only prayed for my wife's healing. That pastor's prayers increased our suffering.

My son, whose daughter has cancer, suffered when a person sent him a book that teaches that when our prayers are not answered, it is because we are not praying the right way. The author teaches that to pray is to argue our case in the courtroom of heaven, and we must learn to operate in the courtroom of heaven if we are to get our prayers released and unlocked. I disagree with this author; he did not draw his thoughts from God's word. The person who sent the book included a letter and signed it, "A friend." The "'friend" sent the book implying that my son's daughter has cancer because my son doesn't pray properly, and the "friend" didn't even sign his or her own name.

Some people have walked away from the church and from God, and even denied His existence because they gained an improper belief about prayer.

A young athlete was injured in an accident and became paralyzed from the waist down. He depended on a wheel chair for mobility. A pastor offered to anoint him with oil and pray for him. The pastor marked a Friday night and promised the young man that if he had faith, he would be healed. The young man called friends and family members telling them, "Saturday, I'll drive my car to your house, jump out, and run to your front door." The pastor brought several church leaders. They massaged the young man's legs with olive oil. Then the pastor shouted, "In Jesus' name, get up and walk." Two men lifted the paralyzed youth from his wheel chair, they let go of him, and he fell to the floor. The praying group left the young man lying on the floor. For over an hour they shouted their prayer, "In Jesus' name, get up and walk." Finally, the pastor said,

"Well, he just doesn't have faith." The group walked out of the house, leaving the young man lying on the floor.

A church leader was traveling in a third world country. He had an accident and an emergency room doctor gave him a blood transfusion to save his life. The blood was contaminated and the man developed AIDS. Church leaders told the sick man, "If you prayed with faith, you'd be healed. There is no place in this church for members who have no faith." The sick man was requested to no longer attend the church where he was once a leader.

Dale and David Weatherford are among my closest friends. Dale shared an experience of prayer abuse in her church.

Dale fell and broke her heel in the summer of 2014. Then Dale experienced chronic pain that spread through her body. It became necessary for her to step down from various ministries in her church. Dale was bombarded with offers of prayer for healing. She eagerly accepted those offers and appreciated the time that prayer warriors spent talking to God on her behalf. But those prayers came with a steep price.

One prayer warrior told Dale, "God is not glorified by your suffering! He suffered so you won't have to!" Another told Dale that the only way she could be in the center of God's will was to be healed. Dale was instructed to pray more, confess more, trust more. Another prayer warrior told Dale, "You will experience full healing if you just visualize Jesus on the cross and repeat, 'By his stripes we are healed.'"

Dale did not experience healing, but she experienced an alienation from several dear friends who had prayed with her for years. They treated her as though she disappointed and failed them by not being healed. The emotional pain of losing close friends added to her physical pain!

A lady struggled to become pregnant. She heard at her church many God-stories about God answering prayer. She heard that if enough of the right people prayed the right kind of prayer, God would answer them. She considered that some of those God-stories were of shallow consequences. For example, a pastor told of his experience. On a rainy day, the pastor prayed for a parking space close to the entrance to the mall, and a parking space opened on the front row. A college football player told his God-story of playing in a football championship game. His team had the ball. They were behind by four points with less than a minute to play. On fourth down, the football player prayed to catch the football and to score the winning touchdown. God answered his prayer and he made the winning touchdown.

For years, this woman took fertility treatments and asked church members to pray for her to become pregnant. After six years of fertility treatments and prayer, she finally conceived. The pastor shared her story as evidence that God answers prayer. The woman and her husband were filled with joy. The baby was born and lived only two days. The experience led this young woman to turn away from her faith and to stop believing in God. Her church taught her that God answers prayers; yet God failed her in her time of greatest need. She wondered, "Does God answer prayers for parking spaces and touchdown passes, but not for barren women and mothers whose babies die?"

What about Christians who daily cry out to God and they only hear the sound of their own voices? What about believers who open themselves up in prayer; and yet, they go to God's waiting room and wait, and wait, and wait? What about believers who feel that God has them on hold or He has disconnected them? It is hard to understand when you have prayed hard, but the answer is "no" and you don't know why. And you may never know why. Do you believe that God is with you even when He doesn't answer your petitions? Do you trust that God's plan for you is better than yours? Is God real and does He answer prayer when He doesn't answer your requests? Those questions can be the ultimate test of trust.

During the time when my wife's health was deteriorating, I ran into a fellow Christian whose wife had spent six weeks in the hospital between life and death. Her health was improving, but she had a long, hard road to recovery.

I asked my friend, "How are you doing?"

My friend answered, "Oh, I'm blessed. God is good. God is good all the time! How are you doing?"

I answered, "It is hard on me to see my wife in declining health. It's harder on me than on her."

At that point, my friend shared about his suffering during his wife's sickness.

Christians who only hear God-stories of joyful blessing from God often feel ashamed to share God-stories of suffering. They may cry themselves to sleep at night but put on smiley faces at church and hide their struggles. The church needs to hear joyful God-stories of prayers answered as desired, and it needs to hear the God-stories of facing undesirable answers from God.

I prepared this book on prayer during a time when God kept giving me undesirable answers to my prayers. My wife's health went into a downward spiral. I prayed for her health to improve; request denied, her health deteriorated. I prayed that she could stay in the house she loved; request denied, it became necessary to move her into assisted living. I prayed for God to show His mercy; request denied, my wife screamed with pain. I prayed for her to be able to stay in assisted living; request denied, it became necessary to move her to a hospice facility.

I shouted my requests to God. I heard silence from God — terrible silence, deafening silence. I listened to God's silence; my heart dried up inside of me, and I could barely stand it. I entered the inner circle of despair.

I experienced the pain described by the palmist David, "When my prayers returned to me unanswered, I went about mourning as though for my friend or brother. I bowed my head in grief as though weeping for my mother" (Psa 35:13-14 NIV).

I'm sharing my God-stories of facing undesirable answers from God, because I'm not the only praying Christian to receive undesirable answers from God. I'm sharing lessons God taught me about prayer, while He was denying my prayer request, hoping others can benefit from those lessons.

BIBLICAL EXAMPLES OF UNANSWERED PRAYERS

- King David prayed earnestly for the healing of his sick son. "David pleaded with God for the child. He fasted and spent the nights lying in sackcloth on the ground" (2 Sam 12:16 NIV). But David's son died anyway.

- Jesus prayed to be spared a violent death on the cross. He prayed, "My Father, if it is possible, may this cup be taken from me. Yet not as I will, but as you will" (Mat 26:39 NIV). However, shortly after Jesus' prayer, He was arrested, tried, and executed.
- Three times, Paul prayed for relief from a recurring sickness that he called a "thorn in my flesh," but God's only answer was, his grace was sufficient for Paul (2 Cor 12:7-9). The thorn in his flesh remained.
- Paul asked the church in Rome to, "Pray that I may be kept safe from the unbelievers in Judea and that the contribution I take to Jerusalem may be favorably received by the Lord's people there, so that I may come to you with joy, by God's will, and in your company be refreshed" (Rom 15:31-32 NIV). God's answer was different than Paul's request. Paul was not rescued from the Jewish people in Judea who refused to believe (Rom 15:31). Paul was falsely accused and arrested, and a mob tried to kill him (Ac 21:27-31). Paul was not allowed to visit the church in Rome with joy and to be refreshed with them (Rom 15:32). Paul was sent to Rome as a prisoner (Ac 28).
- Hebrews 11:35-40 says that many godly people did not get, while they were living on earth, what God had promised. But God considered those people as heros of the faith because they were willing to trust God regardless of what type of answer they got to their prayers.

God said "no" to David, Jesus, Paul, and others. God may sometimes give us a "no" answer, but when He does, He gives us power, strength, and grace through which we can accept His answer.

Unanswered prayer is a perplexing spiritual issue, especially in light of several bold biblical promises that God answers prayer:
- God told the psalmist, "He will call on me, and I will answer him" (Psa 91:15 NIV).
- Jesus promised, "Ask and it will be given to you; seek and you will find; knock and the door will be opened to you" (Lk 11:9 NIV).

Unanswered prayer creates spiritual distress and confusion. Children who become drug addicts, cancer patients, war, famine, divorced church member, church members' children in prison, church members in assisted living or in a nursing home, and church funerals are signs that point to prayer requests not answered as requested. The day I moved my wife into the hospice facility, five other patients arrived. Each of those six people who moved into the hospice facility were signs that pointed to prayers not being answered as requested.

Believers pray on bended knees, opening their hearts to God, asking Him for many things: healing of cancer, a child being freed from drug addiction, a job after becoming unemployed, a buyer for their house in a frozen market, the end of pain, etc. Some prayers will be answered, and the recipients will give thanks to God. The thankful will joyfully tell their God-stories, gratefully testifying what God did. We rejoice thinking about the God-stories we've heard and proclaim, "That is the kind of God we serve!"

But what about the believers who at night cry out to God and the only thing they hear is the sound of their own voices? What about the prayer request they've prayed for many years, and it appears that God has them on hold, if He has not disconnected them. What about when they open themselves up to God and they are placed in God's waiting room? Making sense of prayer not answered as requested is not easy.

PROPER REACTION TO UNANSWERED PRAYER

1. **Understand That Jesus Often Used a Figure of Speech Called "Hyperbole"**
    Our expectations of prayer are shaped in part by Jesus' words in passages like the following, "Truly I tell you, if you have faith and do not doubt, not only can you do what was done to the fig tree, but also you can say to this mountain, 'Go, throw yourself into the sea,' and it will be done. If you believe, you will receive whatever you ask for in prayer" (Mat 21:21-22 NIV).

    It appears that Jesus promised to do whatever we ask, provided we have faith. We read this and other similar promises from the lips of Jesus, and we are confused when our prayers are not answered as we requested. We pray for a friend who is addicted to drugs, and our friend overdoses on drugs; we pray for a family member who is sick, and then attend his funeral; we pray for the safety of our children, and our child breaks a leg in a bicycle accident; we pray for a job to open up for us, and we go for months without employment.

    If unanswered prayer is not the result of our inadequate faith, then how do we explain the fact that our prayers are sometimes unanswered? Perhaps the answer is not found in what we do wrong when we pray, but in our failure to understand what Jesus meant when He said that we could move mountains and have whatever we ask for if we pray with faith.

    Jesus often spoke using a figure of speech called "hyperbole." Hyperbole is an overstatement or exaggeration to make a point. It is a device that we employ in our day-to-day speech. Hyperbole is an unreal exaggeration to emphasize the real situation.

    Some examples of hyperbole:
    - This book weighs a ton.
    - My grandmother is as old as the hills.
    - It was so cold, polar bears wore jackets.
    - She is so dumb, she thinks Taco Bell is a Mexican phone company.
    - This car goes faster than the speed of light.

- That joke is so old, the last time I heard it, I was riding a dinosaur.

By using hyperbole, people make common human feelings remarkable and intense to such an extent that they do not remain ordinary. Jesus used hyperbole. He expressed an unreal exaggeration to emphasize the real truth. Some examples:
- "You blind guides! You strain out a gnat but swallow a camel" (Mat 23:24, NIV). Jesus meant, "You pay close attention to little things but neglect the important things."
- "If your right eye causes you to stumble, gouge it out and throw it away" (Matt. 5:29 NIV). Jesus meant, "Don't look at things that cause you to lust."
- Jesus said, "If anyone comes to me and does not hate father and mother, wife and children, brothers and sisters—yes, even their own life—such a person cannot be my disciple" (Lk 14:26 NIV). The true meaning is a person must put Jesus in first place in order to be Jesus' disciple.
- "Why do you look at the speck of sawdust in your brother's eye and pay no attention to the plank in your own eye? How can you say to your brother, 'Let me take the speck out of your eye,' when all the time there is a plank in your own eye?'" (Mat 7:3-4 NIV). Jesus meant, "Why do you condemn others for small things when you ignore the big things in your own life?"
- Jesus said, "Again I tell you, it is easier for a camel to go through the eye of a needle than for someone who is rich to enter the kingdom of God" (Mat 19:24 NIV). Jesus' hyperbole is easily explained. The camel was the largest animal regularly seen in Israel, and its contrast with the small size of a needle's eye shows the utter impossibility of the effort to squeeze the camel through the needle's eye.

Hyperbole is not deception. The speaker intends the audience to know he is exaggerating to express a particular truth. Jesus spoke in the normal, everyday language used by common people of his culture and time. And just as we normally use hyperbole in everyday language, so did Jesus. Just like we exaggerate and say things like, "This is the worst day of my life", so did Jesus. Jesus used preposterous overstatements similar to the exaggerated "Texas stories," which no one believes literally, but which everyone remembers and understands. The general principle is that hyperbole expresses emotional truth rather than literal truth. We need to scale back the element of exaggeration in a hyperbole and then understand the principle implied. If we take Jesus' words about prayer "hyper-literally," we will become confused and feel deceived. To understand Jesus' words as hyperbole, means we take Jesus seriously, but not always literally.

Return to Jesus' words, "Truly I tell you, if you have faith and do not doubt, not only can you do what was done to the fig tree, but also you can say to this mountain, 'Go, throw yourself into the sea,' and it will be done. If you believe, you will receive whatever you ask for in prayer" (Mat 21:21-22 NIV). Jesus' listeners understood that Jesus was speaking hyperbolically. In normal conversations, they referred to big problems as mountain-size problems. They understood that Jesus was saying that if you have faith and pray, mountain-size problems that seem impossible to deal with can be resolved.

2. **Paul's Response to an Answer to Prayer Different from His Request**
Three times, Paul prayed for relief from a "thorn in my flesh," which was a recurring health problem. God's only answer was, "'My grace is sufficient for you" (2 Cor 12:7, 8). The thorn in his flesh remained. Paul realized that Christ's power was strongest when he was weak. Therefore, he accepted his weakness in order that Christ's power would live in him (2 Cor 12:9-10).

3. **Job's Response to an Answer to Prayer Different from His Request**
"Though he slay me, yet will I hope in him..." (Job 13:15 NIV).

Back-story:
Job made this statement when he was in a worst-case-scenario of pain and suffering. He had lost all his children, his wealth, and his health. His wife ridiculed him and advised him to curse God and die. His friends claimed superior knowledge to Job, and claimed they were speaking God's truth when they accused Job of suffering

because of his sins. Job felt as though his life was over and that his afflictions could bring about his death.

Job's prayers were unanswered and he was experiencing a worst-case-scenario; yet Job declared, "God may kill me with this affliction; however, I will still depend on him because I have no other hope but him." Job had the determination to stick to God, though God should strip away comfort after comfort, and though there should be no respite to his sorrows until Job sunk down in death.

Application:
Job's faith-filled statement has challenged believers to strive for a similar trust in the Lord in the face of worst-case-scenario afflictions. We need a faith where we depend on God even when our problems and suffering are increasing to the point that they could kill us. It is a false faith that depends on God's blessing us with health, prosperity, happiness, and His answering our prayers the way we request. We need a faith where if we experience heart-wrenching unanswered prayers, we will still declare, "Even if God uses my afflictions to kill me, I will depend on him because he is my only hope." That's faith!

4. **Habakkuk's Response to an Answer to Prayer Different from His Request**
"Though the fig tree does not bud and there are no grapes on the vines, though the olive crop fails and the fields produce no food, though there are no sheep in the pen and no cattle in the stalls, yet I will rejoice in the Lord, I will be joyful in God my Savior" (Hab 3:17-18 NIV).

Back-story:
The book of Habakkuk opens with the prophet's complaint to God (Hab 1:2-4). The situation in Judah was chaotic – anarchy, riots, corrupt judges, laws were not obeyed, and no justice existed. Prophet Habakkuk complained that worst of all God was doing nothing about it. God answered Habakkuk that He was working, but the prophet wouldn't believe what He was going to do. God was going to use the Babylonians (Chaldeans) as an instrument of judgment (Hab 1:5-11). Habakkuk questioned God because the Babylonians acted worse than the citizens of Judah (Hab 1:12-17). In Habakkuk chapter three, the prophet looked back to history at

the great acts of God: God overcame the Egyptians at the Red Sea; God brought the Israelites through the experiences of the desert and into the Promised Land; God overthrew the nations of Canaan and planted His people in the Promised Land (Hab 3:1-5). But at the present time, Habakkuk trembled with fear expecting the day of trouble (Hab 3:16). Habakkuk imagined the worst-case-scenario that could happen (Hab 3:17). Then Habakkuk proclaimed, if the worst-case-scenario happened, he would still rejoice in the Lord and find joy in the God of his salvation (Hab 3:18). Habakkuk committed to praising God regardless of external circumstances. Even when God answered his prayer differently than requested, and even if Habakkuk suffered the worst-case-scenario, he was determined to praise God.

Application:
If we were to transpose Habakkuk's terms into expressions which we would use today, we could say, "When I lose my job and my unemployment insurance runs out; when I can't work and am denied my disability claim; when I have no money in the bank but the bills keep coming; when terrorists bomb the bridges and I can't get to town; when there is no food in the store, no fuel in the gas station, no electricity, no job to be had, no available doctor, no available hospital, and no pension for the elderly; yet, in spite of it all, I will have cause to rejoice in the Lord and have joy in the God of my salvation."

We need the commitment that when God answers our prayers in ways that are undesirable to us, and we are experiencing the worst-case-scenario, we will still rejoice in the Lord and find joy in the God of our salvation. We are determined to stay committed to God because of who He is. Our commitment is not dependent on God blessing us or answering our prayers the way we request.

THE BLESSING OF UNANSWERED PRAYERS
Unknown Confederate Soldier

I asked for strength that I might achieve;
I was made weak that I might learn humbly to obey.
I asked for health that I might do greater things;
I was given infirmity that I might do better things.
I asked for riches that I might be happy;
I was given poverty that I might be wise.
I asked for power that I might have the praise of men;
I was given weakness that I might feel the need of God.
I asked for all things that I might enjoy life;
I was given life that I might enjoy all things.
I got nothing that I had asked for,
but everything that I had hoped for.
Almost despite myself my unspoken prayers were answered;
I am, among all men, most richly blessed.

ooo

Responses to an Answer to Prayer Different from Requested

Some of my friends shared with me their reactions to prayers that were answered differently form their requests.

John Ramsey pastored churches in the United States for fifteen years. His wife Cami was his help-mate. Then John and Cami did international ministry with the International Mission Board for twenty-seven years. They lived and worked in Brazil, Bermuda, and Mexico. John's major work was as a seminary professor and pastor. Cami was a homemaker and professor of organ and piano.

In 2004, John and Cami returned to the USA to retire. They completed plans for a new house, and they traveled internationally to see their children and grandchildren. Both were enjoying good health, and the future looked bright.

Four months after returning to the USA, Cami suffered a major stroke and lingered unresponsive for four days. John, their family, and friends gathered at her bed during the four days that Cami was silent. They prayed for her healing. Friends around the world prayed along with them. The family and friends experienced hope of healing during those four days as they prayed. However, something happened on the fourth day that John can't explain. John stood by Cami's bed, and he knew that she was no longer present with him. He knew that she was gone, and he knew that they should stop praying for healing. Later that day, Cami passed away.

John described his grief-journey: "With Cami's death, everything went dark. I literally felt like I had been hit by a Mack truck. My prayers were mostly sobbing as I knelt beside our bed. The days turned into weeks, and the cloud over my mind slowly lifted. Looking back, I don't recall how I prayed. I remember that I did not question God's grace or His goodness. Cami had been His child since her early twenties. I knew that God loved her and that He loved me and our family.

"The weeks and months passed and I moved from the feelings of my life being over, to that of taking up once again the mantle of ministry. A small country church requested that I become their pastor. That church was a therapy for my soul, and the beloved church family did much more for me over the next five years than I ever did for them. They walked me back to living again. And God had another blessing for me. He led me to marry Ann. I am whole again; God has healed my heart, and I praise Him for it."

ooo

In 1982, Wade and Sherry Akins moved to Brazil as missionaries with the International Million Board.

Wade and Sherry were a team and their love for each other showed. Wade pursued evangelistic and training activities. Sherry mothered their three children and created an open home. She hosted meals and meetings. They hosted in their home a weekly Bible study and training for Brazilian Christians and a weekly prayer meeting. Guests in their home testified to Sherry's love for God and for the Brazilians.

After arriving in Brazil, Sherry began to have health problems. In 1992, her health problems intensified and she experienced extreme stomach problems. A Brazilian doctor did a biopsy on her lungs and discovered that Sherry had Scleroderma. She was born with the disease but the disease had developed very slowly. Over time, it turned Sherry's internal organs into something like hard leather. No cure exists for Scleroderma.

Wade had a doctor friend who had been his class mate in high school and university. Wade called his doctor friend, and he told Wade that Sherry had a year to live. But Wade never told Sherry or anyone what the doctor friend said. Wade kept it to himself, lived with the pain, cried a lot privately, and prayed a lot privately.

One night Sherry told Wade that the Lord had revealed to her that He was not going to heal her. Sherry began preparing Wade for her death.

Wade recommended to Sherry that they return to the USA where they had two children in the university, many family members, and personal friends who were doctors.

Sherry replied, "The purpose of my life is to glorify Christ in both my life and death. God has called me to Brazil, and I want to stay."

On Friday December 02, 1993, Wade kissed Sherry goodbye and traveled to teach in a town four hours away. On Saturday morning, Wade was convinced the Holy Spirit told him, "Return home." Wade arrived home at 4:20 p.m. Jason, his youngest son, ran outside the house and told Wade, "Daddy, Daddy, we must get mom to the hospital." Wade went inside and saw his precious wife of over 23 years dead on the floor. She had fainted and died.

Wade experienced a deep, dark, painful, and long grief-journey. Wade said, "That day changed my life forever. I felt lost. I felt like I was in a dark, dark, dark tunnel. I could see a light at the end, but I was on the back end in darkness. I cried. I yelled. I screamed. I beat my hands and legs on my bed. I could not think straight for months. I said things that hurt and offended people. I later went to everyone I remembered offending and asked forgiveness."

Wade said he never asked God "Why?" But, he did ask God to give him a word from the Bible. God answered Wade's prayer by giving him a "promise verse" found in Isaiah 43:2, "When you walk through the fire, you will not be burned; the flames will not set you ablaze" (Is 43:2 NIV).

Wade testified, "In my darkest hours I just claimed that promise from God. I held on to it when I felt I had nothing else. Because of God's Word, I survived.

"The struggle was long, hard, and difficult. The pain was deep and great. The tears flowed but God was with me all the way. He healed my soul-wound. I have a scar but that scar is used to help others who have experienced the death of a spouse."

From his experience Wade learned the following life-lessons:
- Soul-pain is real and we need to watch our words when we know people who are experiencing it. It's often better to just be there and not say anything. Listening is more important than talking.
- The Holy Spirit is the one who will heal the wound in time.
- The Holy Spirit comforts the Christian in his/her deepest hour of need.
- The Word of God is powerful, and God speaks through His Word to give us a personal message to meet our needs.
- God will use our pain to help others.

ooo

Gloria (not her real name) is a performing musician and a popular speaker for conferences and church events. She has experienced a long-term unanswered prayer request. She has never shared her story when speaking to the public, but has selectively shared it with individuals who are also struggling with unanswered prayer requests. Gloria's story:

"'To be or not to be.' That is the famous quote of Shakespeare. A quote that has become my private obsession would be 'To be married or not to be married.' That is the question I've been asking myself going on 30 years. I'm way past ready for the answer!

"I know what I would like for the answer to be – a resounding "yes!". But marriage eludes me. While Paul of the Bible states that singleness is more desirable than marriage; and Jesus, the example of all things perfect, never married during his earthly life, my heart's desire is still wedded bliss. I've crave this to a point of obsession. I have prayed for a husband for 30 years. Soon, I will be 50 years old. I never thought I would be a single 50 year old who has never married. It grieves me to a point that is almost unbearable. I have prayed and prayed and prayed and then, prayed some more. My prayers turned into begging, pleading and crying. Then they became plea deals. I'll do "this" if God will just give me a husband. My prayers turned into shouting, screaming, and throwing things. Ok I only threw a pillow, a shoe and a cup.

"What grieves me the most is that it feels like God just refuses to answer my prayers no matter what. Only He knows the reason why the answer has been "no" up to this point. It's just a painful experience that I never expected to be a part of my journey. What purpose does it serve to keep me single? I beg God to change my heart to the point where I no longer desire to be married but that has never happened. Why pray when God doesn't answer? Well, at least, He doesn't answer the way I would like for Him to. I realize that "no" is also an answer.

"What have I learned through all of this? I still believe that God is good. I just don't always understand His ways – which He said I wouldn't. I have also come to understand that God is not Santa Clause. I don't make my wish list and then on December 25 it magically appears on my living room floor close to my Christmas tree. God answers my prayers the way that He thinks is best. When God doesn't answer me the way I prefer, it forces me to trust Him or discover that I don't trust Him. I've been on both sides of that coin. All I can say is that it is a faith journey and not an easy one but He never promised an easy journey.

"Jesus himself prayed a prayer that was not answered the way He would have preferred. Jesus was in the garden of Gethsemane and He asked the Father to take the cup from him of dying to atone for the sins of the world. But the Father told Him "no". So why should I expect to be any different. If God told His only son "no" then clearly He can tell one of his daughters "no" as well. Maybe one day I will have the same attitude that Jesus had – not my will but yours be done."

ooo

PRAYER ACTIVITIES

1. **Envelopes to Help Group with "Praise, Thanks, Sorry, Please" Prayers**
   Some people are shy about praying out loud in a group. Put three envelopes on a table and label them: (1) Praise – Thanks; (2) Sorry; (3) Please. Let group members write prayers on slips of paper and put them in the appropriate envelope. They should tear up the slips of paper of confessed sins before putting them into the "Sorry" envelope. Check the envelopes from time to time to share in the joy of the "Thanks" prayers and to find out "Please" prayers that are still unanswered.

2. **Prayer Pauses**
   The leader, who is leading a group in prayer, prays a one sentence prayer and pauses for individuals to silently pray private prayers. For example:
   - "Father, we thank you for our church/group, and we ask you to help us know and do your will." *PAUSE for individuals to silently pray.*
   - "We remember those people who are absent today." *PAUSE.*
   - "We remember our friends and family members who are non-believers in Jesus." *PAUSE.*

3. **Hand Prayer**
   Our hand reminds us of people we need to pray for.
   - Thumb: Our thumb is the closest finger to our heart. Pray for those closest to you – your family and closest friends.
   - Pointer: Pray for those who have the right to point a finger at you to guide or correct you – your teachers, bosses, pastors, police, coaches, etc.
   - Middle: the middle finger is the tallest one. Pray for those who have a higher position of authority – our president, governor, government officials, city, county, and state government leaders, mayors, student government officials, etc.
   - Ring: The ring finger is the weakest finger and can not be lifted up by itself. Pray for those who need help lifting themselves up – the sick, disabled, depressed, lonely, unhappy, lost, etc.

- Pinky: The smallest and last finger reminds us to pray for others first and for ourselves last.

4. **Seed Prayer**

   Seed prayer is helpful at the end of a worship service or an event when what was taught is meant to be carried out into daily life. Give each person some seeds and pray that the teaching will grow roots and produce a harvest. For example:
   - God of the soil, speak to each person present today so that your message grows roots and produces a harvest.
   - God of the seeds, may your Scripture become seeds planted in our lives to grow so that our thoughts, our words, our hearts, and our actions will grow a harvest that brings you joy.
   - God of the sower, send workers into your fields that are ripe for harvest.

5. **Praise Offering**

   Incorporate into the time when the church members give an offering of money to offer praises to God. Give people slips of paper and invite them to write or draw something that they praise or thank God for. When the offering plate is passed around, people can put in their money and/or their praise offering into the collection plate.

6. **Confessed Sins In the Trash**

   Each member of the group is given a sheet of paper and invited to write a list of unconfessed wrong-doings. Have a minute or two of silence for individuals to quietly confess their sins to God. Then pass the trash can around, and everyone tears up their notes of confessed sins and puts the pieces in the trash can. If the group is meeting outside, you could put the confessed sins in a metal trash can and set fire to them.

7. **Small Group Prayer Activities**
   - Organize the group in a circle. Let each person share a prayer request. Then go around the circle and have the person to the left or right of each person pray for him or her.
   - Invite people to share prayer requests and have one person pray for all of the requests.
   - Divide the larger group into smaller groups of two to four people and share needs and pray for one another.

- Ask individuals to share only one request at a time. After each request, invite someone to pray for it.
- Have someone write on a white board or poster board prayer requests as they are called out. Then the leader calls out the request one by one. After each request is called out, the group has 20 seconds to pray for it.
- Use the "Love, Thanks, Sorry, Please" plan. Have people pray short one-sentence or phrase prayers after each word is called out.
- Allow a person to share a specific request. The person who made the request moves to the center of the circle. Then, everyone gathers around the person making the request, lays hands on him, and briefly prays for him. Then, the next person shares a request and moves to the middle of the circle and is prayed for.
- Name general needs and have people who have that need move to the center of the circle to be prayed for. For example:
  - People with health needs, move to the center of the circle, and we'll pray for you.
  - People with relationship needs, move to the center of the circle, and we'll pray for you.
  - People with job related needs, move to the center of the circle, and we'll pray for you.
- Instruct the group for each individual to think of one thing he or she would like to pray for and put the prayer request into one sentence. Then each person prays their one-sentence prayer.

8. **Large Group Prayer Activities**
- Invite the large group to divide into smaller groups of from three to five, share requests, and pray for one another.
- Have people who have prayer needs come to the front. Invite all in the larger group to extend their hands, and pray for those in front while one person leads in prayer.
- Invite people with prayer needs to come to the front and kneel. Then individuals from the larger group join one of the kneeling persons and pray for him or her.
- Ask individuals to stand if they have prayer needs. Ask people around those standing to lay hands on them and pray for them while the leader leads out in prayer for all who are standing.

- Plan for classifications of general prayer categories such as physical need, financial need, family issues, emotional needs, job/school issues. Name one of the general needs and invite anyone with that need to stand. For example: "Anyone who has a physical need, please stand." Pray for the group that is standing.
- Divide the large group into small groups and assign each small group a certain issue to pray for.
- Instead of asking people for prayer requests, begin praying and let everyone take their request to God.

9. **Keep a Prayer Journal**

Keep a prayer journal as a computer file or in a notebook. You could begin with a blank journal, writing the date and Scripture at the top, and then write out your prayer. Write out your petitions, your spiritual questions, your heartaches, your struggles, your praises, and your thanks. Pray Scripture back to God and write it out in your prayer journal. Write a letter to God. Be creative.

Then weekly or monthly review your journal entries. This will show you how God has answered your prayers. Your past praises remind you of God's goodness and love for you.

10. **Take a Prayer-Walk**

Prayer-walking is the practice of praying on location. It is a type of intercessory prayer that involves walking to or near a particular place while praying. Prayer-walks are taken by individuals, groups, and even whole churches. One or two people can walk through their neighborhood, by schools, by work places, or places where they are visiting, and pray as they walk.

Some people travel to take prayer-walking tours in other countries. Travelers may walk and pray in places where there is no witness of the gospel, where it is illegal to evangelize, or where the gospel light has faded. Appearing as tourists, those believers cover the location in prayer.

A prayer-walk can be as short as a block or as long as many miles. Prayer-walkers use the five senses — sight, hearing, smell, taste, and touch — to increase their understanding of prayer needs. As they walk, when they have insight, they pray. They walk with open eyes, looking for things to pray for. They are on scene without making a scene. Prayer-walkers may walk unnoticed, but they notice the realities and needs of the community where they walk and the people they see.

Prayer-walkers can use common sense as they walk and observe prayer needs. For example:

- Walking through a neighborhood, they notice a house for sale and pray, "Lord, help these people sell their house and get a fair price for it. Help them find a new location to live and help them adapt to their new location. May the purchaser of this house feel welcome in this neighborhood. If they don't know you, may a neighbor who does know You tell them about Jesus."
- If they walk by a school, they could pray for the teachers and students inside, for their safety and peace, and for the devil's schemes in the school to be thwarted.
- If they walk by an untidy yard and a rundown house, they could pray for the health, both physical and spiritual, of the residents inside. They could also pray that God would raise up volunteers to help those in need.

11. Pray about the News

When you read or hear news on the radio or see a news story on TV, pray for the people involved. Pray for politicians and other national and community leaders who make the news.

12. Pray with a Prayer Partner

Find someone to pray with regularly. Plan to meet at a home, a coffee shop, or hamburger place once or twice a week. Praying with a fellow believer is great for personal accountability.

13. Intentionally Pray while Engaged in Activities that Give You Freedom to Think

A good friend has the habit of going for a walk and praying. He walks to pray, and he prays as he walks.

Often when I'm driving my car, I keep the radio off so I can use the driving time as a time to talk to God in prayer. I like to jog, and I often pray as I slowly run.

When you are engaged in an activity that gives you the freedom to think, you can intentionally use it as a time to pray.

14. Pray the Breath Prayer or Palms Up and Palms Down

The breath prayer has two parts. You inhale on part one and exhale on part two. As you inhale on part one, have the palms of your hands facing up and say, "I receive...." and when you exhale on part two, have the palms of your hands facing down and say, "I release....."

For a group setting: I suggest that people sit with their hands palms up in their laps while they say the first line and take a deep breath; then turn palms down and breathe out as they say the second line.

When I could not sleep at night, concerned with my wife's health crisis or my granddaughter's fight with cancer, this is the kind of praying I did. I inhaled with my palms up telling God what I received from Him and exhaled with my palms down telling God what I was releasing. Sometimes I prayed for one or two hours before sleep came.

- Breathe in your longing for God and your receptiveness to His words. Breathe out your releasing your dependence on yourself.
- Breathe in to focus on Jesus. Breathe out distractions.
- Breathe in your longing for Abba Father. Breathe out dependence on yourself.
- Breathe in trust of the Holy Spirit. Breathe out your fear.
- Breathe in to follow the Holy Spirit's leadership. Breathe out to follow your human nature.
- Breathe in Christ's love. Breathe out His love for another person.
- Breathe in Christ's love. Breathe out your fear.
- Breathe in the breath of God. Breathe out your anxiety and concerns.
- Breathe grace in. Breathe personal frustration out.
- Breathe in the guidance of Holy Wisdom. Breathe out worldly wisdom that will mislead.
- Breathe in a clean heart that will renew a right spirit. Breathe out the sinful nature that gives a filthy heart.

LOOKING FORWARD

I started writing this book in January of 2017, when my wife's declining health made it difficult for her to leave the house. I finished the rough draft the last day of December 2017, eleven days after my wife's funeral. During the year, I cried out to God like I've never done before. However, most of my prayer-cries resulted in undesirable answers. I prayed for my wife's health to improve; however, her health grew worse. I prayed that she could stay in the house she loved; however, it became necessary to move her into assisted living. I prayed for her to be able to stay in assisted living; however, it became necessary to move her into a hospice facility. I prayed for God to show His mercy; however, my wife experienced extreme enduring pain. Invitations came for speaking and training opportunities that I had prayed for. However, I cancelled those invitations so I could have the privilege of being my wife's care-giver. I cried out to God, but His answers were not what I wanted.

During the time when God kept giving me undesirable answers to my prayers, I kept praying, and I studied prayer to improve my prayer life. I didn't choose the journey of being my wife's care-giver. I didn't choose the journey through grief. Doctors and nurses are the healers at the hospital and we want healthy healers to help heal us. But the best healers at church are those who have been wounded but are on the road to recovery. They are "The Wounded Healers."

The Bible's Wounded Healer Manifesto is found in 2 Corinthians 1:3-4. "Praise be to the God and Father of our Lord Jesus Christ, the Father of compassion and the God of all comfort, who comforts us in all our troubles, so that we can comfort those in any trouble with the comfort we ourselves receive from God" (2 Cor 1:3-4 NIV).

God comforts us when we are wounded so we can use the same comfort we received from God to comfort others who are wounded.

I suffered many wounds during the year of 2017 when most of my prayer-cries resulted in so many undesirable answers. But while I was being wounded, God was teaching me many lessons about prayer. It is my desire that sharing lessons learned about prayer while I was being wounded will help me be a wounded healer.

In May, 2018, five months after my wife's death, I was reading through the Psalms and praying them back to God. One day I read, "Be gracious to me, for I am lonely and afflicted" (Psa 25:16 NIV). That day, for the first time since my wife's death, I looked at the pictures she had stored on her computer. Several times I cried to God through my sobs, "Be gracious to me, for I am lonely."

Two days later, I read, "I am confident of this; I will see the goodness of the Lord in the land of the living" (Psa 27:13 NIV). That verse hit me with the impact of a sledge hammer, "I will see the goodness of the Lord in the land of the living." I'm not going to have to wait until I join my wife in death and experience my heavenly birth before I see God's goodness, "I will see the goodness of the Lord in the land of the living." I had found comfort from Paul's words in 1 Thessalonians 4:13 that we do not grieve like people who have no hope. I had the hope of, after my death, being with my wife, and together we would see the goodness of the Lord. But I now have the hope of seeing the goodness of the Lord in the land of the living.

While I'm grieving, I've seen some glimpses of God's goodness, but I am confident of this; I will see the goodness of the Lord in the land of the living.

On Wednesday morning of December 20, 2017, I buried Doris, my wife of fifty-two-years. That afternoon I shared my fear with my sons, daughters-in-law, and grandchildren. I feared that I would become another example of, "There is no fool like an old fool." I know several men whose Christian life I admired, who became widowers and made foolish choices. Some fell into sexual temptations and their indiscretions brought them shame. Several Christian widowers were so lonely that within four to six months they rushed into a new but disastrous marriage.

C. S. Lewis, in "A GRIEF OBSERVED" said, "No one ever told me that grief felt so like fear." For thirteen months after Doris' death, I lived in fear. I experienced fear similar to that of feeling lost in a dark forest without a map or compass or GPS. I had no way to protect myself. I experienced a permanent sense of being afraid.

A couple of weeks after Doris' death, I went to a potluck dinner and one single lady kept touching me. Once, she touched my arm in the exact way as my wife used to touch me. I felt that Doris had touched me! I felt an intense desire to take that woman into my arms and use her body to feel my wife's body. After the potluck, I had uninvited, unwanted fantasies of my taking that woman into my arms and exploring her body in order to experience what I use to feel with my wife. Accompanying the fantasies was the terror of being discovered, losing the respect of my sons and grandchildren, and losing the privilege of ministering as a Christian.

I loved Doris, my wife for fifty-two years. I was lonely, desperately lonely. I didn't like being alone. I feared that loneliness would push me into an undesirable marriage. The apostle Paul said that it is better to marry than to burn (1 Corinthians 7:9), but it is also better to burn than to be burned by a bad marriage.

Months after Doris death, I googled for advice on widowers dating. The basic advice I found was that the widower could go as far as the woman allows, and after a few dates he should expect the woman to remove all boundaries. I am a Christian widower, so biblical boundaries for singles now apply to me. I experienced other unwanted fantasies of being on a date with a woman, being unable to control myself, and my becoming her tempter by pushing her to remove her boundaries. These fantasies were accompanied by the terror of being discovered and being shamed.

I continued to read the Bible and pray. But I seldom felt joy and excitement while doing so. But I realized that the days I skipped Bible reading and prayer, my undesirable fantasies and fears intensified. I followed the advice: when it is hard to read the Bible and pray, work hard at reading the Bible and praying. I knew God was with me because the Bible promises that God is always present with those who love Him. But I didn't feel God's presence. Almost daily, I cried out the words of the psalmist, "Be gracious to me, for I am lonely and afflicted" (Psalm 25:16 NIV). I also cried out, "I remain confident of this: I will see the goodness of the Lord in the land of the living" (Psalm 27:13 NIV). God is good, but I saw few signs of His goodness.

I experienced my soul's midnight hour. God's light was similar to the twinkling of a star on a dark night; it wasn't strong enough to guide me. In years past, I've often felt God leading by giving me desires. But since Doris' death, I didn't feel God-given desires. I made decisions by telling God, "This is the decision I'm making unless you close the door or give me a better choice." For example, I live full-time in a motor-home and I seek work-kamper jobs, where in exchange for a few hours work per week I have a free RV site. Free is better than paying $500 a month. I paid to stay at a RV campground close to Dallas, Texas in order to spend Halloween through Christmas near two of my sons. I applied to several campgrounds close to Dallas and also in the northwest for a work-kamper job. Nothing, but a work-kamper job in Georgia opened up. I didn't feel God leading me by giving me a desire to go to Georgia, but I told God in prayer, "I'm going to the work-kamper job in Georgia unless you close the door or open another opportunity."

Thirteen months after my wife's death, I read 2 Peter, chapter one, "His divine power has given us everything we need for a godly life....For this very reason, make every effort to add to your faith goodness;... knowledge; ... self-control; ... perseverance;... godliness;... mutual affection; and... love" (2 Peter 1:3-8 NIV). I realized, Christ's divine power gives me everything I need for a godly life, but I myself need to add self-control. I realized: Jesus Christ enables me to develop self-control. I remembered that the fruit of the Holy Spirit includes self-control (Galatians 5:22).

At once, I felt the joy of feeling that God was speaking to me! It was the first time I felt God was speaking to me since Doris' death! I felt God was saying: You don't need to fear that you will have no self-control and your loneliness will push you into an undesirable marriage; you don't need to fear that you will be overcome by temptation that you can't resist and be shamed. Jesus Christ and the Holy Spirit enable you to have self-control. You may be tempted but you have the God given ability for self-control. If you yield to temptation or make a bad decision, it will be your choice, not because you were overwhelmed and had no self-control.

Immediately, I was freed from fear. I've not experienced another unwelcomed, uninvited fantasy accompanied by terrorizing fear. Instead of thinking about widowers who played the fool, I intentionally started thinking about widowers who reorganized their lives in a godly manner. On most days, I'm excited to read the Bible and pray, instead of forcing myself to fulfill an obligation. I've felt God leading me by giving me desires. I felt God leading me to stop isolating myself and to get involved in social activities. Someone sent me an e-mail about a church group taking a bus to a Hawaiian restaurant. I didn't know anyone from that church, but I felt the desire to join them, and I'm convinced the desire was God-given. I've had other desires that I've acted on and I'm convinced they were God-given in order to guide me.

For the first time since Doris' death, I'm feeling peace that is accompanied by the absence of terrorizing fear. The psalmist prayed, "Be gracious to me, for I am lonely and afflicted" (Psalm 25:16). I've dropped the last two words and now I'm praying, "Be gracious to me, for I am lonely." My eyesight for seeing the goodness of the Lord is improving. I'm still on my grief-journey; I still have assaults of grief; but I'm accompanied by God's peace.

I am a student of prayer, and I have a lot to learn. I wrote this book about prayer as a fellow struggler in the trenches. I'm struggling; I'm trying to improve my prayer life and to help others to do the same. During the time when God answered my prayers differently than I requested, my confidence in prayer increased. I feel the need to pray more than ever before.

I hope and pray that this book on prayer which I prepared to help me will also help other students of prayer. If God chooses to answer your prayers differently than you request, may this book help you to keep trusting God, keep praying, and keep learning to pray.